# Living Your 'Someday' Now!

# Living Your 'Someday' Now!

**LIFE DESIGN JOURNAL INCLUDED**

IT'S
ALL
ABOUT
WHAT
YOU
BELIEVE

Jo Anne Musolf

Copyrighted Material

Living Your 'Someday' Now!

Copyright © 2015 by Jo Anne Musolf. All Rights Reserved.

No part of this publication may be reproduced, stored in a retrieval system or transmitted, in any form or by any means – electronic, mechanical, photocopying, recording or otherwise – without prior written permission from the publisher, except for the inclusion of brief quotations in a review.

For information about this title or to order other books and/or electronic media, contact the publisher:

Jo Anne Musolf

www.joannemusolf.com

joanne@joannemusolf.com

Library of Congress Control Number: 2015920983

ISBNs:

Print: 978-0-9969623-0-8

eBook: 978-0-9969623-1-5

Printed in the United States of America

Cover and Interior design: 1106 Design, Phoenix AZ.

*Dedicated With Love To*

*Frank "Moose" Musolf*
*My Dad*
*Who Taught Me To "Think Blue"*

*Jenny Musolf*
*My Mom*
*Who Taught Me Self-Reliance*

# CONTENTS

Acknowledgments. . . . . . . . . . . . . . . . . . . . ix

Introduction . . . . . . . . . . . . . . . . . . . . . . xi

## EXPLORATION

Chapter 1.
What's Your Trigger to Change? . . . . . . . . . . . 3

Chapter 2.
Who's Really Taking Your Journey? . . . . . . . . . 15

Chapter 3.
What Beliefs Have You Been Lugging Around? . . . . . 31

Chapter 4.
Why Do You Keep Ending Up at the Same Place? . . . . 47

Chapter 5.
Which Path Will You Choose? . . . . . . . . . . . . 61

## LIBERATION

Chapter 6.
    Stop! Don't Do Anything . . . . . . . . . . . . . . . . . 75

Chapter 7.
    What Do You Really Want? . . . . . . . . . . . . . . . . 79

Chapter 8.
    Why Don't You Already Have What You Want? . . . . . . . 93

Chapter 9.
    Metaphorically "Lobotomize" Limiting Beliefs . . . . . . . 99

## CREATION

Chapter 10.
    What Else is on Your Bucket List? . . . . . . . . . . . . 119

Chapter 11.
    Write an Empowering Story . . . . . . . . . . . . . . . 133

## TRANSFORMATION

Chapter 12.
    Getting Comfortable with Being Uncomfortable . . . . 153

Chapter 13.
    Preplanning Support to Keep You on Course . . . . . . 165

Chapter 14.
    Living Your "Someday . . . " Now! . . . . . . . . . . . . 177

Life-Design Journal . . . . . . . . . . . . . . . . . . . . . . . 181

About the Author . . . . . . . . . . . . . . . . . . . . . . . . 243

# ACKNOWLEDGMENTS

If my life were encapsulated in a book, its title would definitely be "Jo's Jaunts." By far my most interesting jaunt to date has been writing "Living Your 'Someday' Now!" My mother always said I was born with a suitcase in my hand and that same suitcase was constantly packed as friends and family around the world opened their homes to me so I could write surrounded by beauty, peace, and love. I can only say, "Thank you, thank you," to Jo Ellen and Paul Nevans, Jeanina and Herbert Franck, Mark Le Doux and Bill Albinger, Ellen Powers and Frank Miller, Carla Spreng and Drew Webb, and dear, dear Aunt Rosie and Uncle Bob Olson.

Every professional butt kicker, which I've always been, needs to be nudged and prodded along, too. For that I bow in gratitude to my long-time friend Glenn Swain, the best "ex" ever; to Karen Leff, who makes me laugh like no one else; to my morning coffee group: Judy Vincent, Wes Izer, Ross Shannon, Marsha Hendrix, Norm Wagner, John Laing, Tim O Malley, David Wood, and Michael Melnick; to

Pam Wilson with the same everything—birthday, house, clothes, and medical aches and pains; and to Stacy Glorioso for schlepping me on trips and tolerating my constant talking.

In this book I talk about having support people to keep you sane and on track. For that I thank Tia Stokes, my insightful, nurturing, and wise friend who always brings me back to my truth; Naomi Bartz, whose curiosity always leads to a plethora of fun activities and conversations; Ellen Antill, who has shared her wisdom and insight from the first moment we met; and to my Amigas: Bobbie "Jo" Lombard, Mary Pat Thompson, Chris Franke, Lindy Kemp, Lois Noltemeyer, and Vila Seefeldt.

The mechanics of writing this book took far more guidance than I ever imagined. My patient, kind, thorough, and encouraging editor, Susan Waterman, kept me on course and off the ledge. Saul Bottcher of Indie Book Launcher was most generous in sharing his thoughts and feedback as I struggled through uncountable title ideas. And Ronda Rawlins and Michele De Filippo at 1106 Design, who were beyond patient with me, and who put it all together to make it look good.

To every client and program participant, I'm deeply honored that you invited me along on your personal jaunts and life explorations. You have filled my heart and made my own personal journey luscious and joyful.

# INTRODUCTION

Clients have usually spent years sharing their "Someday Life" or their "Someday Business" story with family, friends, and business associates. In the telling of their "Someday" story, they paint a detailed picture of an idealized life where they have an amazing new career, a new relationship, less chaos in business, a plan for retirement, better health, more money, a sense of purpose, increased self-esteem, less sameness and more adventure. But no matter how often they've vowed that, "Today's going to be the day I take control, change what needs to be changed, and make it happen," they're not any closer to living that happier enhanced life or having that successful business experience; they're only more practiced in telling their wishful-thinking story.

I've been no different. I had all the best intentions, felt motivated, energized and ready to change. And I started. But, like my clients, I engaged in numerous, creative rationalizations for not staying on the journey to the end. Years ago, writing this book was one of those thought-about-but-not-finished journeys. Until…

## My Trigger-Nudging Story

Friends, coaching clients, and seminar participants had all heard me talk about "my book on the drawing board." But none of those conversations ever resulted in producing one word on one page. Then one day Josh Hornick, my insightful, call-my-bluff coach, said, "Eight months ago you mentioned you were going to write a book. How's that coming along?"

Eeks! When did I tell him that?

"You're right, Josh, I did say that and I still intend to get it written:

- **But** I'm really busy with clients right now. (Truth: I live alone and have no less than five hours of free time most days.)
- **But** I have to take care of my aunt and uncle. (Truth: They live three hundred and fifty miles away.)
- **But** I'm only mentally creative in the morning. (Truth: I come up with pretty damn good ideas after a short nap in the afternoon.)
- **But** I'm committed to being healthy and can only exercise in the morning, but that's when I'm also the most creative. (Truth: If someone calls at 3 PM to go hiking, I'm out of the house in a minute.)
- **But** I don't know how to type and no one can read my writing. (Truth: There are at least a kazillon people who can read handwriting as bad as mine and who make a living typing up gibberish.)

## Introduction

Within seconds I had rationalized my lack of action with a litany of believed-to-be-true excuses. I was astounded by the speed of my responses, but then I shouldn't have been. After all, I've been repeating those "buts"—and variations of them—for more than forty years. They were hardwired into my brain. So it's no wonder I regurgitated them without ever asking myself if they were still true. That conversation left me feeling prickly and I couldn't shake it off. For the next two days I was agitated and kept hearing a nagging voice telling me, "Jo Anne, just write the damn book."

It turns out that Josh's question was the trigger I needed to ask myself why I still had not put pen to paper. The next morning I got up a half-hour early, grabbed my journal, and asked myself the same question I ask each client when they rationalize their reasons for backing off from a long-desired goal or a dream, "Jo Anne, what beliefs do you have that, if they were totally expunged from the story you tell yourself about yourself, would free you to get up tomorrow and begin your book?"

These were the beliefs I came up with:
- I can't be a writer without a degree in writing and I have a math degree, for God's sake.
- I can't author a book about transformation until my own life is totally "fixed."
- I must be in a creative mode every hour of the day.
- I'll need hours of free time to write.
- I can't ask for solitude in order to write.
- I can't work out in the afternoon or evening.

- I must be able to type.
- I must have good handwriting.
- I have to be intensely focused because writing is hard.

Since I believed each of these to be true, the obvious conclusion was, "I can't possibly write a book." End of problem, end of dream.

But, but… what if I didn't believe, "I'm not a writer?" What if instead, I trashed that whole list of beliefs, replaced them with really good ones and created a brand new story? What could I do and say tomorrow that would be different and would free me to not only start but actually finish a book? What were my possibilities? Now what? Just say the words, the beliefs are gone, the book is done, and life is good? Is it that easy?

Actually it is and it isn't.

"Living Your 'Someday' Now!" is both a book and a life philosophy. As you read this book, you'll learn how to make well-thought-out, purposeful changes so you can, once and for all, live the life you've just dreamed about. In addition to teaching a process, this book is also a soul-searching endeavor to uncover, unleash, and upgrade your long-held stories and beliefs. It's also a journey to a magical, lovely, fulfilling, satisfying, and contented life. In its four sections—Exploration, Liberation, Creation, and Transformation—you'll learn how to make sustaining, transformative changes which I define as getting to the right place, at the right time, with the right people, and having the time, energy, health, and resources to enjoy it when you get there.

Introduction

On this journey you'll become skilled in the process of designing thoughtful, sustainable, and permanent changes instead of blindly reacting to quick, temporary fixes. Unlike with past efforts to change, you won't rush toward your goal at supersonic speed. In contrast, this transformational journey will be a step-by-step self-directed walk. Instead of passively riding along while someone or something outside of you determines your direction, course, and speed, this time you'll decide where you want to go, how you get there, when you start, and how fast you travel. On this journey the pace of the walk is just as important as the destination.

This four-step process is applicable for individuals, teams, businesses, organizations, boards of directors, communities, and institutions. In this book I'll mostly focus on individual transformations; but every step along this journey to change is adaptable to any situation or group.

I know you've read many self-help and business books by the people I call the "birthers" and "bring-forthers" of new philosophies backed by old wisdom. Authors like Eckhart Tolle, Pema Chodron, Ken Blanchard, Deepak Chopra, Stephen Covey, Maya Angelou, John Wooden, Julia Cameron, Wayne Dyer, Sandra Bender, Oprah Winfrey, etc. have helped to transform the thinking and lives of readers and students alike. Their books put forth theories and asked thought-provoking questions about how to have a better-feeling life, a prosperous business experience, solve an ongoing problem, or make a sustainable change. While reading their books, you probably experienced many "aha's." Then a few days later you probably put the book down and, although you meant to, you never acted on any of those insights. And, just as likely, after a few weeks, you forgot them altogether.

I'm not a "birther." But I am a clarifier, simplifier, storyteller, and teacher. Always have been. Before I embrace a new thought or philosophy, I need to feel how it applies to real-life situations that relate to my heart, my soul and my mind. Only when that new philosophy connects to all three, do I get "it." It's my hope that my interpretation, clarification, and simplification will help you see and feel your way on your journey to living your "Someday" now!

It is also my hope that this time the aha's you experience and the correlations you draw with your personal life won't be put on the back burner with the intention of pulling it out at some point in the future. At the back of this book starting on page 181 you'll find a Life-Design Journal to use as you make the connections between what you're learning and your unique personal life. Remember this is a self-directed walk. If you truly intend to make this the time you'll enhance your life or business, then you need to do it differently. You'll be coached to write out your answers to the questions posed in chapter sections and to note the reactions you have to the concepts and suggestions presented. Be aware of thoughts like, "I don't want or have time to do this." or "This is crazy, unnecessary, and I don't believe it's going to make any difference." Those thoughts are the mirrors you'll need to get a

## Introduction

clearer picture of what's really stopping you from living a joyful life or having a satisfying business.

When you're finished with this book and the supportive journal work, you will have created a Life-Design guide to keep you focused and on track until you get to your Someday-Ideal Destiny. If you're reading this on an e-book or if you'd rather use a hard copy of the Life-Design Journal independent of the book, it can be downloaded from www.Livingyoursomedaynow.com

# EXPLORATION

# Chapter 1

WHAT'S YOUR TRIGGER TO CHANGE?

*From My Journal:*

Don't know why this came up right now. When and why did I make the decision to quit teaching so many years ago?

I now remember the exact moment I made that life-altering decision. I was getting dressed for work and heard the radio announcer say that the retirement age for teachers had been increased to seventy years old.

"Seventy? You're kidding me," I remember saying out loud.

I'd been in school or teaching school for twenty-five years. And when I heard that I could continue teaching for another forty-five years, I thought, "That'll be a total of seventy years spent in education; and I only picked education because Mr. Berendt, my high school math teacher who was frustrated by my incessant talking said, 'Miss Musolf, what do you intend to do with your life?' I sassed back with, "I want to be a math teacher just like you." He retorted, "If you become a math teacher, I'll eat the book." And so, to show him, I did.

I thought about that radio announcement all the way to school and for the next few days. For the last year or so I hadn't been satisfied with either my life or teaching. My strong need for adventure and having new life experiences just weren't being fed. I didn't know what I was going to do next. But what I did know was that there was no way I would take another job that was structured and curtailed freedom and flexibility.

That spring I quit teaching and packed my Chevy Suburban, which I lived out of for the next nine months as I traveled around the United States. Prodded by my need for surprise and adventure, my plan was that when faced with making a decision between two possible roads or highways, I'd always veer towards the road with the least amount of traffic.

That radio announcement was my trigger to, literally, explore and travel a new path.

## *The Journey to Transformation Begins*
**Setting:**
> Jo Anne's office. Sun streaming in the window. Phone rings.

**Jo Anne:**
> "Hi, this is Jo Anne. How may I help you?"

**"John" says:**
> "I need to (fill in the blank) my (fill in the blank) Now!"

| | |
|---|---|
| Change | Business |
| Revolutionize | Leadership style |
| Transform | Career |
| Fix | Life |
| Figure out | Relationships |
| | Health |
| | Retirement |
| | Social life |
| | Purpose |
| | Passion |

**Jo Anne answers:**
> "Now? Hold your horses."

By the time I get this call, John has tried every which way to change or solve this same challenge. Why didn't any of John's time, energy, money, and spirit-consuming attempts ever get him what he wanted? He wasn't lazy, incompetent, or delusional. Nor did he lack motivation, desire, or willingness to see it to the end. Pure and simple in the past John, like most everyone else, tended to approach all his journeys to change with the same itinerary and schedule: start here, go there, and do it as fast as humanly possible. But a journey, whether for personal or business reasons, to a thoughtful and permanent change is not about getting to the destination in record time.

**A journey to a transformative change is about getting to the right place, at the right time, with the right people, and having all the time, energy, health, and resources you need to enjoy it when you get there.**

### *What's Your Nudging Story?*

Change is inevitable. No way around it. Something is always going to be fluctuating and shifting in both life and business. The charts on pages 9 and 10 list many dynamic areas of life and business that, at one time or the other and for one reason or another, necessitates the need to alter the direction of your life. Some life and business changes you'll initiate and others will seem to come from out of nowhere and blindside you. No matter where it comes from, each urge to change begins with a nudge. Sometimes it's a kick-in-the-pants nudge and other times it's a quiet whisper. The first segment, Exploration, begins by identifying the nudge that's pushing or pulling you to make a life or business transition.

### *What Would You Like to Change?*

But, before you articulate your nudge, take a few minutes to step back and mindfully view your life from a birds-eye, overall perspective.

## What's Your Trigger to Change?

How would you answer this question: "If you could have it all, what needs altering or total revamping in your life?" Another question to ask is, "If I told my family, friends, and co-workers to be totally honest, what would they say I needed to change in my life or business?"

> *Life-Design Journal page 182: Review the charts on pages 9 and 10 and list each life and business category where you'd welcome an alteration or total change.*

I'll bet, when you reviewed your list, your first reaction was that your entire life needed a complete house cleaning and that as long as you're focusing on one area, you might as well attack everything at once. Whoa! That's too much to tackle at one time. Slow way, way, way down. Remember, you're only going to move one thoughtful step at a time. If you give in to the temptation to "clean everything in your house at once," your focus and energy will get pulled in every direction and all you'll end up with is many "starts" and no "finishes." It didn't work before and it won't work now. So, narrow the list of things that need changing down to two or three of the most urgent or enticing categories that are calling to you for attention.

> *Life-Design Journal page 183: Which two or three of those you just listed do you feel the strongest need or urge to change?*

Next, from those two or three areas, which one would be "The One" for you? Since nothing changes in a vacuum, as you thoughtfully move through each of the four Segments, each area you've listed will eventually be altered and transformed. But for now just focus on "The One."

*Life-Design Journal page 183: What is your "The One" and why?*

## Life Changes

| Job/Career | Personal | Mental/Emotional |
|---|---|---|
| New Career | Marriage/Divorce | Self-Esteem |
| Retirement | Empty Nest | Connectedness |
| Promotion/Demotion | Death | Bored |
| Layoff | Home Environment | Life/Work Balance |
| Office Politics | Education | Personal Freedom |
| Communications | Relocation | Sense of Security |
| Ex-pats | | |

| Physical/Health | Relationships | Spiritual/Religious |
|---|---|---|
| Aging | New Relationships | Purpose |
| Attractiveness | Family/Children | Connection |
| Injury/Disability | Friends | Peace |
| Nutrition | Parents | Faith |
| Stress | Community | Meaning of Life |
| Quality of Life | Neighbors | |

## Business Changes

| Employee | Markets | Sales |
|---|---|---|
| Employee Turnover | Geography | Downsizing |
| Dissatisfaction | New Markets | Outsourcing |
| Hiring | Customers | Expansion |
| Layoffs | | Acquisitions |
| Reorganization | | Divestiture |

| Financial | Technology | Strategy |
|---|---|---|
| Sales | Manufacturing | Change of Vision |
| Profit | HR | Competition |
| Sources of Funding | Systems | Regulatory |
| Leverage | Integration | Environment |

## Every Transformative Event Has a Trigger.

And "trigger" is the spot-on word that describes the event, word or feeling that produces that nudging reaction that your life, or some part of it, needs to change now! At this very moment! But, if truth be told, that need for change has probably been simmering for a very long time. Nonetheless, you feel compelled to do something "right now or else!" The way you've been living and how you feel about it just doesn't work for you anymore. You want "it" to stop.

So, what's triggering your desire to create a change right now? Did your boss raise her eyebrows when you suggested an innovative idea for the department? Did you see an ad for the Greek islands and feel a strong impulse to pack your bags? Have you noticed the permanent dent in your couch from too many hours of watching TV? Have you reached your frustration or pain threshold? Are you cranky, snarky, or moody? Or, on the other hand, is there something so enticing and attractive that you just can't live another moment without it? What is pushing or pulling you to move forward?

> *Life-Design Journal page 184: Why now, at this particular time, do you feel compelled to change your life or business? Describe your triggering experience.*

## *Is Your Trigger Painful or Pleasurable?*

There are only two compelling reasons to change. One is pain and the other is pleasure. When I use the words pain and pleasure, I'm referring to all the nuances of each—sadness, happiness, confusion, joy, disgruntled, weariness, anger, love, any feeling of discontent, or any feeling of hopefulness.

Painful triggers are stronger butt-kickers than pleasurable triggers. Pain pushes you to engage in immediate action: a supervisor tells you to increase sales or start looking for another job; a doctor threatens that if you don't lose weight you'll get diabetes; a company memo reminds you that you have three months until retirement; yesterday's business forecast indicated that your company's product is quickly becoming obsolete; or an ultimatum is given that "this relationship needs to change or else."

Pleasurable triggers, on the other hand, attract and magnetize you to action: You take dance lessons as a way to spend more time with your partner; you work to increase sales because you want the money to go to Greece; you and your spouse want to retire in five years so you can start that African import store you've always dreamed about. Pleasurable triggers don't stimulate the forceful got-to-do-it-right-now urgency that occurs with painful triggers. And, because of a lesser degree of urgency, pleasurable triggers are easy to ignore and usually put on the back burner, where they often stay. On this thoughtful journey to change, however, you'll give pleasurable triggers as much attention and time as, in the past, you only gave to painful triggers.

> *Life-Design Journal page 185: Pushed or pulled? Are you looking forward to this change, being forced to endure it, or feeling neutral about it? Write a few words about this feeling.*

## *What's Your Level of Urgency?*

With clarity about what's triggering your need to change, the next question to ask yourself is, "How compelled am I to do what I have to do to get what I say I want?" Does it feel imperative that you do something right now—like in the case of an impending job loss, or a medical diagnosis? Can it wait for a day or two? A few months? Another year? Motivation is always at its peak the first few days after you decide to turn things around. But how truly driven are you, at this moment, to invest time and energy into enhancing your quality of life or to solve a reoccurring challenge?

> *Life-Design Journal page 185: On scale of 1-10, with 10 being very motivated, what's your level of urgency? Write more about why you chose that number. Don't judge the number—it's only information.*

## What's Your Believed Level of Staying Power?

Here's another question whose answer will expand your awareness: "Do you believe you'll stick with this journey, inclusive of all its ups and downs, until you get to its end?" In other words, do you really believe that this time you'll stay the course to do what it takes to get to where you want to go?

> *Life-Design Journal page 186: On a scale of 1-10, how likely are you to stay with this journey to the end? Why or why not? Again, don't judge the number you chose—it's just information.*

Don't judge yourself if, in all honesty, you ranked yourself low on any one of these scales. Keep in mind that your past failed attempts to change are not proof positive of your future endeavors. In the "Liberation" segment of this journey, you'll learn how to release non-supporting beliefs about these numbers and any other measurements or rankings that, in the past, prevented you from starting and staying on course to the end.

Let's recap. So far, in the Exploration segment of your journey you've:
- Identified the area where you want to make the first change
- Pinpointed your trigger
- Decided if you were being pushed or pulled
- Measured your level of urgency
- Honestly gauged your believed-to-be level of commitment.

The next thoughtful step of "Exploration" is a walk down memory lane, where you'll reacquaint yourself with the people, circumstances, and events from your past that created the makeup and matrix of the person, you, who will be taking this journey.

# Chapter 2

## WHO'S REALLY TAKING YOUR JOURNEY?

*From My Journal:*

Coffee + bread = dunking!
Yesterday when Karen and I were having our coffee and a bagel she said, "For God's sake, you have cream cheese on that thing. Do you have to dunk everything in your coffee?"
"I always dunk bready stuff in my coffee," I told her.
"Why?"
"I don't know, I just do!"
But now I wonder, why do I do that? When did it start?
I was five or six years old. It was Saturday morning so that meant that Dad had walked to Wieninger's Bakery and brought home a dozen hot, fresh, hard rolls. Grandma sat me on her lap, buttered a Kaiser roll with cold, hard butter and let me dunk it in her coffee. I remember that the coffee tasted nasty. But I loved sitting on her lap and dunking. It was our Saturday ritual. When there was only one small bite left, Grandma would give me the last piece of roll to dunk and say, "Okay, Honey, it's all yours." To me that was absolute love and comfort.
When I got older the ritual changed to Saturdays being about cleaning house, doing yard work, and finally, when all the chores were done, going out to play. Grandma moved out and there were no morning walks for hard rolls, no coffee, and no dunking.
Sitting in a cocoon of comfort on Grandma's lap was the last time I had coffee until I was twenty-one and a first-year math teacher at Cudahy Junior High. It was my first day of teaching and I nervously entered the teachers' lounge. Everyone there was drinking coffee. Instantly, I had a taste-bud memory of how nasty that stuff was. But I didn't want to be a conspicuous newbie, so I forced myself to pour a cup of coffee and then without thinking, grabbed one of the donuts sitting in the middle of the table and started dunking. Once I dunked I felt comfort and started to relax.
For me my comfort formula is "coffee + bread + dunking = personal comfort."

## *Who Are You?*

As you start this self-directed journey, let me ask the following questions: "Who are you today? What are the stories and characterizations you use to portray who you are—to yourself and others?"

When I ask clients these questions, most off-the-cuff answers are usually a recitation of gender, age, personality traits, and things they like and don't like. But, as you'll discover in the next few chapters, the whole of who you are is more profound, much deeper, far more impacting, and has been disremembered for a very long time. It is precisely those long-forgotten stories and why you believe you are the way you are that are the keys to whether you'll allow yourself to live a deliberate, happy life.

## *Your Life-Defining Play*

To help you reacquaint yourself with the character traits, complex motivations, and hidden depths of the "you" who's starting this journey, I'll use the analogy of a play. In this play, which you'll title, "My Life-Defining Play," you'll cast yourself as its Lead Actor.

Let me remind you of the components of any play:

- **Lead Actor:** the star or protagonist
- **Defined Setting and Context:** where the play occurs, the era, the economics of the time, the environment, etc.
- **Supporting Cast of Players:** other actors who are there to define and flush out the character of the lead actor
- **Character Development:** the physical aspects, personality, nature, and idiosyncrasies of each actor

- **Script:** the story and dialogue that's cast in stone and forwards the actors and their actions to the unalterable and predetermined ending
- **Direction:** specified, non-negotiable actions and non-actions, emotions, movement, and responses
- **Costumes:** the framing of each character and how they visually appear to their outside world
- **Ending:** never changes—good, sad, uplifting, engaging, sorrowful, or miraculous.

Once the script is written, the set constructed, the costumes designed, the actors selected, and the lines memorized, rehearsals begin. At this point in the production the director assumes total control and dictates the movement, timing, emotions, and actions he deems necessary to forward his vision of the message of the play. Countless rehearsals and hundreds of shows later, the actors don't have to think anymore. Their words, actions, and the predicted outcomes are habitual and flawless. And, day after day, the story of the play ends the same way.

Here's a synopsis of my Life-Defining Play from birth to about twenty-five years old as an example. As you read the details, keep in mind that the story of my life-defining play was the story I repeated to myself, and everyone else, for more than thirty years. It was that story that set the parameters of how I lived my life and the opportunities I either embraced or ignored until many years later when I set out to purposely and thoughtfully release the weight of my history from my baggage.

◦ ◦ ◦

### "JO ANNE'S LIFE-DEFINING PLAY"
### Act One
### *Birth and the Learning Years*

**Setting:**

"Jo Anne's Life-Defining Play" is set in Milwaukee, Wisconsin, in 1946. Milwaukee is a city with many ethnic cultures and influences (German, Polish, Italian, Bohemian, Hispanic, Irish) with harsh winters and humid summers. Bay View, our small neighborhood, is blue-collar, friendly, and close. Most men work in factories and most women work in the home.

The Catholic Church and grade school I will attend are close to home. Humboldt Park is a block away and has an ice-skating pond, tennis courts, and a big band shell. We are also "lucky" to live two miles from Lake Michigan and, as I am repeatedly told, "You are within walking distance of **everything** you could possibly want."

We never lock our doors—don't even have keys.

**Supporting Cast of Actors:**

Dad, Mom, Grandma, Uncle Joe, Aunts Alyce and Rosie, and brother Roger all living in the same small house

**Character(s) Development:**

**Grandma**—Never went to school; never learned how to read or write; we shared a bedroom until I'm fourteen. She is my biggest supporter at home.

**Mom**—She's extremely smart, but dropped out of school after eighth grade to help support her family; works in the home and her claim to fame is having the cleanest house on the block.

**Dad**—He's kind, patient, positive, and loved by everyone. He works his butt off at two jobs: one in a factory and the other in a produce store. He always looks tired but never complains.

**Aunts and Uncle**—Unlike Mom, they enjoy life and laugh a lot.

**Roger**—My only sibling is three years younger than I. He became the much-loved son.

**Mom and Grandma**—They have a constant battle about what constitutes a clean house and who's in charge. Grandma sneaks behind Mom's back to do my chores so I can go play. Mom, who believes in the value of a clean house more than playing, is aggravated by her actions.

**Script and Direction:**

I am directed (taught) that:

- All older people must be obeyed and respected no matter what they do or say.
- "Our kind of people" don't live in big houses and never will.
- Floors must be hand-scrubbed twice a week or others will think we "live like pigs."
- No matter what it is, all household or yard chores are the responsibility of everyone who lives in the house.
- "No one leaves to have fun until everyone can leave to have fun."
- "We're surrounded by any and everything you can expect to get because that's just who we are."
- "Red has always been your favorite color."

**Act Two**

**Emerging Individuality: Youth and Teens**

Layered on top of what I've been scripted to think, believe, say, and do as a child, I start to be influenced outside of the constraints of my immediate family and environment. Teachers, clergy, friends, activities, TV shows, movies, and music enter the story, each adding another dimension to my personal characteristics. This is also the time of "teen challenges"—raging hormones and, what I perceive to be, a nagging mother.

Mom is not healthy and spends weeks in hospitals and facilities. Since she isn't home and Dad works two jobs, I'm responsible for Roger, and all household chores and fix-it problems in the house. By the time I'm fourteen I'm super competent and irked by anyone who suggests I can't do something or that I may need help.

My best friend in high school is Cindy Hunn. It's her mom who teaches me that wearing rollers in my hair to shop downtown is not appropriate. When the guy who sits in front of me in chemistry class runs his comb down the hair on my leg, I learn that women shave their legs. My high school friends and I all watch "American Bandstand." So I encourage Roger to choose "Fabian" as his confirmation name. Yeah, I really pay for that one.

The biggest outside-the-family influence is Mrs. Case, my geometry teacher, who strong-arms me to go to college. Since Grandma never went to school and Mom only finished eighth grade, no one ever gave it a thought that college could be my next educational step, much less, that it might be advantageous for my future.

## Act Three
### Adult Years to Age Thirty: A Synopsis

I become a math teacher who actually ends up teaching in the same school as Mrs. Case.

## Who's Really Taking Your Journey?

I live close to the family home because I'm "within walking distance of everything you could possibly want."

I spend Saturday cleaning because I don't want anyone thinking I "live like a pig."

At this point, I believe myself to be beyond super-competent and usually say, "No thank you, I can do it myself." Since I've convinced everyone that I can do it myself, no one offers to help me anymore.

Many clothes in my closet and most presents I receive are red because "it has always been her favorite color."

I told my third grade teacher I'd never get married and she replied, "Oh Jo Anne, of course you will." I empathically replied, "No I won't!" For my thirtieth birthday Aunt Alyce sends me the wedding afghan she knits for each niece with a note saying, "I'll never live long enough to see you get married."

## Living Your 'Someday' Now

### COACHING NOTE:

What number did you choose to indicate the likelihood that you'd finish this journey? This is one of the crucial junctions in your journey to change where you have to make a decision. Are you tempted to put this book down, saying, "I just don't have time for this." Or will you make a new choice by taking fifteen to twenty minutes to sketch out your own Life-Defining play?

> *Life-Design Journal page 187: Use the prompting questions from the play categories listed on the following pages, to fill in the specifics of your Life-Defining Play. As you continue this process, you'll start remembering other experiences that defined your early life. Return to this journal section to add new insights as they occur.*

## Your Turn:

_____'S LIFE-DEFINING PLAY
*Insert Your Name*

**Lead Actor: You**

Cast yourself in the role of "Lead Actor" in this Life-Defining Play. The specifics of your play—its setting, its story line, its directors, their dictated actions, and the other cast members—predisposed the direction, success, and satisfaction of your life and business journeys to date.

**Setting and Context:**

Before your stage entrance, the day you were born, the context and setting of your play were already in place: the time in history, the neighborhood, the economics of your home and country, family politics and religion, and the environment. Was the setting during the Depression, in a college town, on a farm, in a tenement or a mansion? Did you have to share a bedroom with many siblings or did you have servants? Was there an extended family present? How did your family earn its money? Was there a religious or political belief? What educational level did the others in your life achieve? How was the division of labor between men and women determined? Was there a park, a pond, farmland, or concrete parking lot to play on?

**Supporting Cast of Actors:**

The supporting actors in your Life-Defining Play were the people who reared you, fed you, taught you and disciplined you. Were they parents, grandparents, relatives, adoptive parents, foster parents or caretakers in an orphanage? Others might have been teachers, friends, family, relatives, clergy, neighbors, and maybe even the friendly clerk at the A&P. Each one entered your play with their own unique back story and experiences as influencing factors.

Who were the "others" in your play? What impact did they have on you? Did you like them, love them, or were you afraid of them? What did they look like and why was that memorable?

**Script:**

Your parents, teachers, neighbors, and friends were all co-writers of your first script. They told you exactly what to say and do, when to say and do it, where to say and do it, and how to say and do it. Remember, though, that each of them had been, in turn, using elements of scripts that were written by their parents, teachers, and clergy.

Did you hear "Children should be seen and not heard?" Were you told to keep your new newfangled ideas to yourself? Or were you encouraged to speak up and be heard? What did your mother stress as being important or what did she tell you to stay away from? Your father? Your teachers? Your clergy? What words or statements are floating around in your psyche that either encourage or stop you from taking the next step?

**Director(s):**

The directors had a strong vested interest in your performance and how it impacted **them** and the other characters. They decided what behaviors, actions, and costumes were appropriate for your character. You were told what to believe, what to like, what to accept, what to eat, what to study, what to read, what to wear, and even whom to like and not like. You were guided, and at times even harassed, until you did everything **they** believed was right or important and that made **them** comfortable. What's more, you were expected to perform this way, every day, every time.

Although they used words to direct you, how else did the important people in your life direct you? Did they pick up a ruler and slap it in their hand to make you toe the line? Did they keep "pink slips" on their desk for you to see? Did they give you a hug or positive acknowledgment every time they saw you? Did they make a favorite cake on your birthday? Did they teach you to play tennis even after working two jobs?

**Character Development:**

The script and the directors' choices shaped the individuality, personality, and nature of your character and the other actors in your play. What is the disposition of your character in your Life-Defining Play? Did you end up being obedient or sassy, outspoken or shy, a book reader or an athlete? Did you like unusual foods or would you only eat hamburgers and pickles? Were you one way in the family and another way in the outside world, known as happy, quiet, adventurous, creative, smart, a thinker, a troublemaker, or a tomboy?

**Costumes:**

Consider the clothing (costumes) you wore and the costumes of the other influencers in your life—both positive and negative. What assumptions did people make about you based on their first impression? Were they right? Did you wear clothes that were hand-me-downs or were they stylish and expensive? Did you wear one outfit in front of your parents or employees and another as soon as you got out the door? Was your hair long or did you have a perennial crew cut? Blue jeans and boots or khakis and penny loafers? A baseball cap or a head scarf?

**Play Ending:**

Each and every component of your Life-Defining Play was designed to lead to only one possible ending. If one actor, one line, one experience, or one aspect of the setting or back story had been scripted or directed differently, you would have had an entirely different ending. Is there one "ending" you keep living? For example, are you the one who always does all the work? Are you painfully insecure about money, feel tremendously guilty about sex, have never liked your co-workers, or seem to always end up with lazy employees?

## *Impact of the Story You Tell*

As a coach and trainer whose lifelong passion has been to help people make lasting changes and achieve sustaining happiness, I'm cognizant of the immense impact that clients' stories have on how they're currently living their life or running their business, and on what alterations and changes, if any, they'll be open to in the future.

As I hear their stories, I actively listen to their interpretation of:
- Why they believe they are the way they are: "No one in my family was athletic."

- Why they believe they must do what they do: "The economy is lousy so I'll wait to get a new job."
- Why they believe they can't get what they want: "Our kind of people don't live in big houses."

Each person or business I've coached has repeated the story of their Life-Defining play hundreds of times. So, it's no surprise that they, and everyone who's repeatedly heard them, believe that those stories are, without a doubt, absolutely true. But are they really true? And how did they evolve? And, most intriguing, can they be changed?

**COACHING NOTE:**

*Example of Business, Team, Organization, or Board of Directors Life-Defining Play*

*Although the above analogy of the Life-Defining Play is used for personal life changes, I use the same play analogy when working with business entities: Business-Defining Play, Board of Directors-Defining Play, Department or Team-Defining Play. I encourage each executive, board of directors, division or department to think of their business or team as the lead entity in a play. What was the setting when the business, board, or department was first developed? What were the culture, era, and environment of business at that time? Who were the other players at that time? What direction came down as "must-dos"? How did the play end each day?*

*We'll then explore the company's beginning, what were the owners' dreams the day they opened their doors, what business* beliefs did they bring to the organization, and what phases have they lived through to get to this stage in the company's existence. A crucial inquiry is, "What's the repeated company line regarding change: "It's always been done this way; don't upset the apple cart," or "We've always been an innovative company; let's see what else we can do?" Studying any business or organization entity using this play-analogy provides a truly deep perspective when planning for future transitions. Without considering the history, the players involved, and the unconscious beliefs that each brings to the table, the journey to transform the company or organization will be all uphill.

# Chapter 3

## WHAT BELIEFS HAVE YOU BEEN LUGGING AROUND?

*From My Journal:*

Wrote about two hundred sentences yesterday and then got stuck searching for the right word. In that brief moment, my *You're-Going-to-Make-a-Fool-of-Yourself* voice said, "Jo Anne, are you crazy? Writing a BOOK is a big deal. Don't you realize that even natural-born writers don't write books? People might actually read it. And unless you get it perfect, which you won't, they'll criticize it, and make fun of you. And you will be so-o-o embarrassed. And they'll think you're stupid and you won't be able to show your face anywhere."

Wow—double wow! Let me get this right. Do I believe that? Do I honestly think that if I make a mistake I'll be considered a fool and that I'll be so embarrassed that I won't ever show my face? Why am I giving the word "book" the power to make or break how I feel about myself?

Why isn't it just a book? When did it stop being a fun experience and morph into an ugly have-to-or-else-my-life-will-be miserable job? The word "book" seems to scare me, so what if I didn't think of it as a "book?" What if I just think of it as an idea to put together some thoughts that I have into words. And that those words will fill a certain number of pages and those pages may or may not be valuable to someone else?

I know that "book" and "writing process" have no absolute meanings beyond what I give them. So why then am I choosing to give them such defeating, life-crushing meanings?

## What Beliefs Have You Been Lugging Around?

*"What probably distorts everything in life is that one is convinced that one is speaking the truth because one says what one thinks."*
—Sacha Guitry

### Beliefs and Meanings

**Your personal beliefs, along with the unique meaning or judgment you assign them, are the predictors of how you'll experience your life.**

In the context of making permanent, sustainable, and uplifting changes, I define "belief" and "meaning" as follows:

**"Belief"** is your personal conviction that something is true.

**"Meaning"** is the feeling, significance, value, or definition that you attach to a belief, an event, an idea, an action, or a word.

You have thousands of beliefs. You have beliefs about your beliefs and everyone you know has beliefs about your beliefs. Your beliefs are intertwined, overlapping, and intricate. And, since you've repeated them time and again, they have become an ongoing, seemingly permanent part of your story.

Your beliefs are the assumptions you make about yourself and others. They control what you think about. They determine what you think is true and what isn't true. They define how you expect things to be. They're the basis for the places you'll go and the risks you're willing to take. They determine the people you'll let support you and the people whose input you'll ignore. They also have power to determine the out-of-the-box experiences you're willing to try, the movies you'll see, the books you'll read, the TV stations you'll watch, the classes you'll take, and the restaurants you'll patronize. Your beliefs can be supportive or limiting. They can be long-held or recently learned. They can lead you to exciting and satisfying futures or keep you stuck in your ruts. They define the depth and breadth of your dreams.

**Simply put, your beliefs—along with the unique meaning or judgment you assign them—predict how you'll experience your life.**

And, obviously, until those long-held and often forgotten beliefs are examined and, if need be, altered or released, you'll continue to have the same outcome and the same degree of satisfaction or dissatisfaction you've always known. There's no way around it. To alter or transform the course of your life or your business, or your health, it's imperative that you become consciously aware of the beliefs shaping your existence.

Read this list of common beliefs and mentally check off any that you own:

- I'm smart.
- The Democrats/Republicans are right.
- I'm creative.
- My boss is a control freak.
- No one makes money in this economy.
- I'm too old.
- I have a lovely voice.

## What Beliefs Have You Been Lugging Around?

- I love talking to strangers—they're like a new adventure.
- These employees are all stupid.
- I'm not smart enough to do that, I was never good with numbers.
- I'm not tall enough, short enough, or thin enough.
- I can't speak in public or to anyone in authority.
- I'm a procrastinator and am always late.
- If my parents were wealthier, my life would have been better.
- I need to have a date, spouse, or friend in order to travel.
- I'm a good problem solver so I'm sure I can figure this out.

If you believe you're a good problem solver, you probably don't freak out when things don't go as planned; and since you don't need to be in complete control, you'll take more risks; and because you take those risks, you'll have an interesting and expansive life. Similarly, if you believe you're a procrastinator, you can bet that something will always "magically" happen causing you to be late with a deadline. And because you're always late completing projects, you'll never be considered for a coveted promotion.

> *Life-Design Journal page 194: Begin listing your beliefs—you'll add to this list as you proceed through future chapters. Include both the obvious and the obscure: rules must always be obeyed, never jaywalk, a messy house is a sign of a lazy person, older women shouldn't wear their hair long. In this "Liberation" segment of your journey you'll decide which life-defining beliefs you want to hold on to and which ones you want to boot out.*

## *A Brief Course on Beliefs*

Most people live their life by default. A widespread mindset is, "It's just how we are, just how they are, and just what will happen. End of discussion!"

- "I've always been a 'worker bee.' I can't possibly take that promotion to management."
- "The economy sucks and there are no jobs. So I'll never get to live in my dream house."
- "The world is in chaos and is going to get worse. We need to arm ourselves."
- "Our leaders are ineffectual and there is nothing we can do about it. So it doesn't make a difference if I vote."
- "The education system stinks and it's only going to get worse. Our future is bleak."
- "I'm 65, twenty pounds overweight, and not rich, I'll never find a woman to love me."

All out of your control or due to someone else???

How did you come to believe that you're lovable or not well-liked; going to be financially secure or would always be struggling to pay bills; destined for a spectacular future or damned to relive the less-than-desirable life of your parents; good or bad, attractive, smart, interesting, athletic, liked a particular food, or were bound by current circumstances for the rest of your life?

How did these preprogrammed, in-your-soul, seemingly cast-in-stone beliefs about how you're destined to experience the rest of

## What Beliefs Have You Been Lugging Around?

your life become your beliefs? Were they coded in your DNA? Nope, not a single one of the many beliefs you own that predict how you experience your life today existed the day you were born. So, if they weren't coded in your DNA, your brain, or your cells, where did these life-controlling predictors come from? Well, they came from one of three life occurrences: programming, exposure, or experience.

### *Programming*

As you think back to your Life-Defining Play, it's obvious that your core beliefs were etched in your psyche by parents, family, teachers, supervisors, clergy, and others who appeared in your story. Based on what they were taught to believe they, in turn, told you what to believe. And because they were the "adults"—the directors of your play—you embraced those beliefs.

**Parents:**
"People like us don't live in houses like that."

**Teachers:**
"Music is the basis for a happy life."

**Clergy:**
"To stay on good terms with God, don't ever question these rules."

**Family:**
"I don't care if your uncle is mean, you be nice to older people."

**Friends:**
"Those brainiacs are losers; if we skip school we'll be cool."

## A PROGRAMMED BELIEF ADOPTED FROM MY FATHER
### "Think Blue."

*Every August there was a huge family picnic for Grandma's birthday. Thirty aunts, uncles, cousins, and assorted family and friends would gather at Sheridan Park for a whole day.*

*Because Milwaukee's summer weather was never predictable, "picnic day" didn't necessarily mean we'd actually have that picnic. When Roger and I woke up to find it cloudy and looking like rain, we'd start whining, "Is the picnic going to be rained out?" "Where will we roast the hot dogs?" "Will Glenn and Bobbie still come from Waukegan?" "What about Grandma's presents?"*

*And my father, the world's most innately positive person, would always say, "Don't worry, honey. Just go to the front window, keep looking at the sky and 'think blue.' Once you see enough blue to make a Dutchman's pair of pants, the rain will go away." So I'd stare out that window and "think blue" until a little patch of blue would appear amongst the clouds. And it worked—year after year. The weather would hold out long enough for us to have our picnic. Always!*

*I never doubted that changing the weather was possible just by "thinking blue." If my father said it was possible, then of course I believed it. As the years went by, "think blue" was the thought and mantra I used whenever it looked like what I really wanted might somehow get "rained out."*

### What Beliefs Have You Been Lugging Around?

> *Life-Design Journal page 196: What did the adults in your life teach you to believe? Pull ideas from the "Script" of your Life-Defining Play on page 190. If you still own those beliefs, add them to your belief-list on page 194.*

## *Exposure*

As tempting as it may be, the adults who populated your early years can't be credited or blamed for all your beliefs. You acquired a whole other set of beliefs that were a reflection of the era and the environment you lived in. That exposure dictated the books you read, the creative ideas you had, the TV shows you watched, the music playing in your house, the things you heard your parents talk about, whether you lived in a rural environment or smack-dab in the middle of the city, and the chores you had or didn't have to do.

Was your family Protestant, Catholic, Jewish, Buddhist, agnostic, or atheist? Were you exposed to classical, country western, or rock music? Were you raised in the Great Depression, a moderate recession, or the good times? Did your parents take you on exotic trips or was a walk to the local pond to go fishing sold to you as a great adventure? Each exposure shaped a "leaning" toward or against the viewpoint, the tenets, or the hype being presented to you.

> *Life-Design Journal page 197: What beliefs or leanings did you adopt due to the era and/or environment you were raised in, for example, during the Great Depression, the sixties, post 9-11? If you still own them, add them to your belief-list on page 194.*

## *Experiences*

Added to the beliefs you adopted from programming and exposure are those morphing out of your unique life experiences—some resulting from repeated occurrences and others the result of a one-time, impacting event.

**Repeating experiences:** These beliefs were assimilated from seemingly innocuous experiences —a word, a look, a comment—that, at first, were barely perceptible. Then the experience occurred again and again. It finally got your attention and you had a feeling about it. You judged it and decided if you liked it. You gave it meaning and created a belief about it.

At some point the initiating event didn't need to be present. All you needed to hear was a **word** (silly, stupid, math, IRS) or smell an **odor** (cabbage, gin, fresh bread) or notice a **look** (a glare, a shake of the head) or read a **noun** (mom, boss, teacher, supervisor) or see a **number** (1939, 65, 9/11) and you experienced an immediate gut reaction which developed into another belief.

**Impacting experience:** These beliefs resulted from memorable one-time-only events that in some way profoundly affected you.

You asked a teacher a question and were laughed at. Thereafter, you never questioned anyone in authority.

You were learning to ski and fell down. Your buddy said, "What's wrong with you? It's easy." Being embarrassed, you retorted, "I'm just not athletic." So you never attempted another sport again.

You invited a pretty girl to the prom. She condescendingly said "No." Twenty years later you're still not asking attractive women for a date.

What Beliefs Have You Been Lugging Around?

## AN IMPACTING BELIEF ADOPTED FROM MY MOTHER

*One Sunday on a ride with my family, Dad drove along Lake Shore Drive where the Milwaukee beer barons owned huge mansions. I was too young to be impressed with the size of the houses, but I just loved the trees on their property and the view of Lake Michigan. I remember saying, "Some day I want to live there." Mom, who didn't know I was referring to the trees and water, said, "Jo Anne, people like us don't live in places like that."*

*That was that. When Mom said what she said, I accepted that because we were who we were, I would never live amongst trees on the shores of a body of water. One innocuous out-of-context comment from a person, I had no reason not to believe, impacted my choices about where I could live for over twenty-five years.*

> *Life-Design Journal page 197: Which words, looks, comments, smells, titles, or numbers cause you to have a spontaneous gut reaction? Can you extrapolate the belief behind that reaction? What impacting experiences affected your life? What beliefs resulted from those impacting experiences? Add these beliefs to your list on page 194.*

No matter how you acquired them, your beliefs form an invisible boundary around your life. They are interwoven in your current story and define the breadth and depth of your experiences. They determine what you perceive, what you expect, what you're wary of, and what excites you. But keep in mind, as influential as they are, they weren't there to begin with and they can be reshaped.

## *Conscious and Unconscious Beliefs*

If asked what you believe, **conscious beliefs** are the ones you'll articulate. You may or may not know where you got them but they're readily accessible and you consciously own them.

When I meet clients for the first time, I ask the obvious question: "What do you want to achieve, do, or change?" After they answer, my next question is, "You're a smart person, so if you know what you want, what's stopping you from already having it?" Their answer to that question quickly reveals their conscious beliefs. They'll share why they can't have it, don't already have it, who or what is in the way of having it, or why it will be so very hard to get it. Each of their answers stems from some belief they have about themselves, society, the economy, medical conditions, the current administration, age, or their family situation.

- I want to change careers and be an artist, but artists never make money.
- I'd like to work for community changes but politicians are just plain crooked. So I'll be beating a dead horse.
- I'll never get the promotion because my boss doesn't like me. So I guess I just need to suck it up and be satisfied.
- It's impossible to get a date with a decent woman because they only want someone wealthy.

## What Beliefs Have You Been Lugging Around?

- I can't get a divorce because my family just loves my wife.
- I'm too old or I'm too young. I'm too much of something and not enough of another.

> *Life-Design Journal page 198 If asked, "Why can't you do what you say you want to do?" what would your immediate answers be?*

According to scientists, 90% of our beliefs are **unconscious beliefs**. You can't immediately articulate them, can't readily say where or who you got them from, and aren't consciously aware that they're determining your life's destiny, but by God you hang on to them.

When you're introduced to someone for the first time, do you ever wonder why you have an adverse reaction to him or her? Why do you gravitate toward being around older people? Why do you say you don't want to travel to China, Europe, Mexico, or Yellowstone Park, yet you've never been there? How do you know you'll never be financially secure, or that you'll never marry? Why do you always settle for having less?

> *Life-Design Journal page 198: Do you have an instinctive reaction to a person, event, idea, smell, etc.? What is the reaction and where does it come from? What is the resulting belief you own?*

## *Beliefs Morph Into Truths*

All beliefs, both conscious and unconscious, whether from programming, exposure, or experience, morph into your **truths**; your believed truths predict every single choice you'll make. Once your beliefs become deeply rooted, you forget they were made up and you start claiming them as **absolute truths.** You're swear-on-a-stack-of-bibles convinced that your beliefs are true. Even in the face of contradictions, you're 100% sure you're absolutely right.

A without-a-doubt absolute truth? I don't think so!

## *Most Beliefs are Not Absolutely True*

When I Googled for an authoritative explanation of what constitutes an absolute truth, I read, "Absolute truth is defined as inflexible reality, fixed, invariable, unalterable facts. For example, it is a fixed, invariable, unalterable fact that there are absolutely no square circles and there are absolutely no round squares."

A less-often quoted, but no less knowledgeable authority, is my morning coffee group. On any day in this eclectic group of eight, someone is an expert in or has had some experience to shed light on the conversation-du-jour. When I asked them, "What are some absolute truths that everyone in the world agrees on?" an enlightening discussion ensued.

Someone jumped in with the fact that Phoenix's current 110° is unbearable, but Norm said, "Not if you're freezing your ass off on an iceberg." Marsha offered the word God. But then someone responded that not everyone believes in God. Another chimed in,

## What Beliefs Have You Been Lugging Around?

"The current economy absolutely sucks." Ross, our banker, said, "Not if you own an inexpensive fast-food restaurant."

"There is always day and night," said John. But Judy responded, "Except in Alaska when Barrow has twenty-four hours of sunlight around the summer solstice. And the region above the Arctic Circle has twenty-four hours of darkness." Someone then offered that gravity always goes downhill but David, our scientist, pointed out that in Wisconsin, there's a spot where water runs uphill. Father Wes, our in-group priest, summarized it best by reminding us how often siblings have contradictory stories about the same family event, each swearing it is the "truth."

In the end, the only absolute universal truths everyone could agree on were those that were scientific definitions, like circles and squares are different shapes, 32° Fahrenheit is the freezing point, and the Earth revolves around the sun. But any belief that had a personal meaning, emotion, or judgment attached to it could not, by definition, be an absolute truth.

Listen, I'm not advocating that you give up truths that you hold dear or that offer life-enhancing stability. What I'm asking, though, is before you make any decisions to change, look at your truths with a new set of eyes and a new spirit of heart. Some truths might not be quite so true anymore, some might need revision, and some might need to be released altogether.

> *Life-Design Journal page 200: What are your truths? What beliefs, philosophies, and tenets govern your life?*

At this point in your life, you've owned your stories, beliefs, and truths for so many years, they're hardwired in your mind. Recall the play analogy where actors who, after years of repeating the same lines and actions, don't have to think about what they're going to say or do next. Like those actors, your "life script" has become mindless and routine. And it is this mindless repetition that's guiding you to the life you're living at this very moment with the same ending, day after day after day. If you're not content with any aspect of your ending, consider editing or deleting the stories and beliefs preventing you from leading the kind of life you really want.

Before you start "liberating" your beliefs, let's look at the logistics of how you perpetuate and fuel your story so you keep ending up at the same place even though you passionately say you want your life to be different.

# Chapter 4

WHY DO YOU KEEP ENDING UP
AT THE SAME PLACE?

*From My Journal:*

Last night I was at Aunt Rosie's sniffling over another boyfriend issue. I said, "and the worst part is that every time he pisses me off I eat a pint of ice cream." She said, "You always liked ice cream, even as a baby."

"Really? Even as a baby?"

"You were only a couple of months old and Milwaukee was shut down by the big snowstorm of 1947. No one could get to the grocery store and the milkman couldn't get to the house. Your mom called the doctor asking what she should do. He asked if she had ice cream and when she said she did he told her to give you diluted, melted ice cream.

After that, whenever you cried, you got diluted ice cream in a bottle. When the streets were finally plowed and milk could be delivered, your mom found that whenever you were really sobbing, and a bottle of milk didn't quiet you down, all she had to do was feed you melted ice cream and you fell right asleep."

No wonder I turn to ice cream every time I'm unhappy.

*A man is literally what he thinks, his character being the complete sum of all his thoughts.*

—James Allen

## *Road Map to Destiny*

"What were you thinking?"

*Watch your* **thoughts,** *for they become your* **words.**
*Watch your* **words,** *for they become your* **actions.**
*Watch your* **actions,** *for they become your* **habits.**
*Watch your* **habits,** *for they become your* **character.**
*Watch your* **character,** *for it becomes your* **destiny.**

—*(Anonymous)*

## *Your Thoughts*

According to the research of Dr. Fred Luskin of Stanford University, a human being has approximately 60,000 thoughts a day, with 90% of these being repetitive. Most of those 60,000 slip in and out of your mind and have no effect on your experiences or your life. They're just observations floating through you mind: *She's wearing blue. It's 3:00 PM. The sun is shining on the plant. That's a dump truck.*

Yet other thoughts, because of the unique meaning you ascribe to them, stir up feelings that you then label as delightful, sad, happy, loving, distasteful or worrisome. Some of those thoughts propel you to a new future and yet others stop you right in your tracks: *It feels chaotic in here. That coffee smells good. His shirt is so-o gaudy. This town is boring. Her red coat is beautiful. Chicken soup reminds me of Grandma.* But, make no mistake, your thoughts directly determine the scope and satisfaction of your life now and of every phase or destiny yet to come.

## *Your Thoughts Lead to Your Words*

To express your **Thoughts** you use **Words**. And as Rudyard Kipling noted, "Words are the most powerful drug used by mankind."

**Words** are everywhere: billboards, radio, Internet, emails, texts, books, TV, videos, and music. They're the conversations we hear in our heads and those we encounter in stores, restaurants, movies, schools, churches, temples, and ashrams.

**Words** are the tools you use to communicate your **Thoughts** to others. They're how you explain ideas and concepts, and how others interpret what you say. To write your **Thoughts** in a journal, you use **Words**. To explain yourself to your boss, or your spouse or kids, or the committee, you use **Words**.

- Boss says, "I need to see you in my office."
  You hear Words.
- Terry asks, "How was your day?"
  You describe it with Words.
- Doctor says, "How are you feeling?"
  You answer using Words.

Why Do You Keep Ending Up at the Same Place?

## *Your Words Lead to Your Actions*

You take **Action** or you don't take **Action** based on the **Words** you use.

*"I don't like to sweat"* probably excludes you from a day's hike.

*"Young employees are just plain lazy"* suggests you won't consider hiring someone younger who's a whiz with electronics and can get the work done in half the time.

*"I absolutely love Italian food"* will propel you to shop for gourmet pasta and peruse recipes for new Tuscan dishes.

*"I'm not pretty"* determines the clothes you buy, the makeup you'll try, and the entertainment venues you'll attend.

*"I don't have a degree"* prevents you from applying for a dream job or imagining a scenario where you'll make a difference in the community.

## *Your Actions Lead to Your Habits*

When you repeat an **Action** (or a **Thought** or a **Word**), you create a **Habit**. And, here's where it gets interesting; most long-held **Habits** eventually become unconscious.

ಌ ಌ ಌ

**A Friend's Unconscious Habit**

*Yesterday Pam, who had owned my house twenty years ago, was helping with dinner. I wanted to mount a sign on the garden wall and she offered to do it. She opened a drawer and said, "What did you do with the scotch tape?" Without thinking, by habit, she went right to the kitchen drawer where she had kept the scotch tape twenty years ago, but where I now stored soup ladles.*

◈ ◈ ◈

### *Your Habits Lead to Your Character*

Your **Character** is the aggregate of features and traits that form your personality and individual nature. If asked, "Tell me about him. What's he like?" the person answering will use descriptive words to portray your unique **Character**.

When considering your sister, your boss, your spouse, your father, your co-worker, or your friend, you will generally think about them in terms of the traits describing their nature.

| | |
|---|---|
| He's kind. | She's lazy. |
| He's inflexible. | He's unapproachable. |
| She's a caretaker. | She's not a risk-taker. |
| He's demanding. | He's a tyrannical boss. |
| She's easy-going. | He's honest. |

### *Your Character Leads to Your Destiny*

Put your **Thoughts**, **Words**, **Actions**, **Habits**, and **Character** together, repeat them day after day, year after year, and guess what happens? You keep living out a story ending that never changes—your **Destiny**. But remember, the **Destiny** you're living is not the irreversible result of circumstances beyond your control nor is it the same for everyone with the same set of circumstances.

Although lengthy, read the following two illustrations, one business and one retirement. Notice how the choice of thoughts, words, actions, habits and character determines the diverse destinies lived by each person.

◆ ◆ ◆

### THOUGHTS ---> DESTINY
### A BUSINESS EXAMPLE

Tim and Greg both have an MBA from the same prestigious business school but work for different companies. They're both about fifty-five and each has twenty-five years' executive experience. Recently they were each asked to lead their department through the economic recession.

### Tim:

**Thoughts:**

"Here we go again. The Democrats/Republicans have gotten us into this mess and now I'm supposed to make changes. I just got these people doing things the way I want them to and now I'm going to have to start all over. I'll have to reduce my staff and then who's going do the work? I sure as hell am not."

**Words:**

- "It's a never-ending struggle. Why can't things just remain the same so I can glide under the radar for four years until my retirement?

- "I'm going to have to dictate a new strategy to these know-it-all youngsters in my department. I know they won't listen, they never do.
- "They're going to hate it when I demand they take on additional projects requiring even more time at work. They're just lazy."

**Actions:**

Tim meets his friend Sarah for drinks after work. Sarah is his sounding (i.e., complaining) board because she's also tasked with facilitating economic changes in her company. They knew this was coming and for the last three weeks have commiserated about how unfair and hard it all is. At work, Tim is short with his staff and complains about every little thing. At home he is testy and not easy to live with. When he watches the news before bed, he gets agitated, angry, and can't sleep.

**Habits:**

Tim has stopped talking to anyone who does not agree with his assessment of this situation. He eats alone in his office and has not gone to one birthday luncheon in the past year. Because he's "sick and tired" of this whole situation, he's stopped going to the gym for a game of basketball with his buddies. Instead, he leaves work and rushes home for a few glasses of wine and "leave-me-alone" time.

**Character:**

Tim has always been known as "the last person you'd want to share a new idea with." He wears the same old brown suits and white shirts day after day. You can expect him to finish a well-defined project. But don't expect him to come up with creative solutions should the project hit a snag. His family went on a California vacation this year without him because he doesn't like the hassles of the new airport security regulations and would rather stay home than "deal with those people."

**Destiny:**

Tim is never assigned any interesting projects. He isn't asked to travel to the company office in China because his boss believes that requires more flexibility then Tim projects. Lately, he chooses to sit home while his wife and kids go to the movies. Tim's biggest concern is that he thinks his boss, that new young guy, might try to get rid of him. He's fifty-five and knows, that at that age, he'll have a devil of a time getting another job.

## Greg's Story in Comparison:

**Thoughts:**

"Well isn't this going to be an interesting challenge? How can we save money and jobs and still serve our customers? I think I'll tap into my younger staff's creative juices. Since they've recently graduated from business school, perhaps they have some ideas I'd never even think of."

**Words:**

- "Let's think of this as an opportunity for growth. I don't have all the answers so I'll need your help as we move forward.

- "I'd like each of you to create a list of ten ways that we can save money in our department, ten ways we could make our products and services better, and ten things you'd do if you had to be responsible for growth."
- "No ideas are off limits."

**Actions:**

Greg takes an hour or so every day to study companies that experienced growth spurts during a downturned economy. It's been almost thirty years since he finished his business degree, so he asked a few of his youngest employees to dinner to discuss what they learned regarding similar situations.

Because he knows that sometimes you learn just by "showing up," he and his wife walk around town looking at both large and small businesses for ideas. Now, especially at this time, he meets weekly with his Transition Coach for her assistance creating and facilitating successful changes in his department.

**Habits:**

Greg loves new projects because they're an opportunity to create and be adventurous. He likes to vary the kind of sports he plays, the restaurants he goes to, the network news stations he watches, and the places he and his family go for vacations. He loves meeting new people and always stops at a coffee shop in whatever towns he visits to "hang" with the locals.

**Character:**

Everyone comes to Greg with new ideas. Just being around him makes others feel good. He's a great listener and a wonderful mentor. His staff especially likes the way he asks questions before he jumps to conclusions. You can always be sure that Greg has your back.

**Destiny:**

The bosses are watching how Greg leads this project. They have great hopes that he'll create a template for expansion and change that can be used in the company divisions worldwide. As a matter of fact, they asked him to represent the company at a conference in Paris next fall. His kids love his fun ideas and how he encourages them to explore and experience new things. Greg is always looking forward and can't wait to see what the next twenty to thirty years will bring.

## THOUGHTS----> DESTINY
## A RETIREMENT EXAMPLE

Liz and Sue are both sixty-six years old, both recently retired from long-held careers, both are in good health, still attractive, and look years younger than their age. Notice how each approaches retirement using the beliefs formed by her personal story and life experiences.

### Liz:

**Thoughts:**

Liz thinks that being sixty-six is old. And absolutely everyone she's talked to that's retired has some sort of illness. She thinks, "When you're old, life should slow down so you can protect your fragile body and waning life. It know it won't be long before my body fails me, too."

**Words:**
- "Let's go to the early movie. We can avoid the rush-hour traffic, be home by 8:00, and get comfortable in our sweats.
- "Thank goodness that at our age we don't have to think about sex anymore.
- "I'm too old to learn all that computer and iPhone stuff.
- "I don't travel much anymore because I want to be near my doctors."

**Actions:**

Liz will predictably suggest brunch or a daytime activity when you call. She donated her work clothes and now only wears "age-appropriate" clothes. When away from home, she'll use a pay phone because "those cellphones are just too damn complicated." Although she'd like to have a male companion to do things with, she doesn't stay open to meet anyone because of "the sex thing."

**Habits:**

Liz takes a slow, leisurely walk around the park each morning. She never pushes herself. She eats at the same restaurants close to home "because that area of town isn't safe and besides, those are ethnic restaurants and their food is spicy. It's just better to eat at home."

**Character:**

Liz's friends know her to be predictable and reluctant to step out of her comfort zone. They think of her as a nice woman but they're never surprised by anything she does.

**Destiny:**

Liz is not invited to any event involving spontaneity, physical activities, or starting after 8:30 PM. Her life takes on the demeanor of slowing down and sameness. Her friends are generally older than she and together they spend time playing afternoon card games.

## Sue's Story in Comparison:

**Thoughts:**

Sue considers sixty-six just a number and thinks of retirement as a non-stop recess.

**Words:**

"Let's go to the early movie so we can get a quick dinner and then go listen to that new jazz group. Maybe we'll meet some really fun men and go dancing. I'll text you with times and places."

**Actions:**

Sue always comes up with creative adventures. She signed up for salsa lessons and plans to go sea kayaking next summer. Her friends call her a "Party-in-a-Bag."

**Habits:**

Sue gets up each day and runs five miles to train for a half-marathon. Each morning she puts on makeup and earrings because,

"You never know when someone will call." Each Monday morning she checks online to see what's going on in town for the week. One especially fun thing she does is to invite friends to visit each of the city's top twenty-five designated restaurants each year.

**Character:**

Sue has friends of all ages and they know her as someone who is "up" for anything. They can always call Sue at the last minute and she'll throw something on and meet them. She's fun, whimsical, smart, and open.

**Destiny:**

With so many interesting things going on in her life, Sue's "dance card" is filled. She's constantly engaged in new adventures and always contributes fascinating topics for dinner conversation. She truly has a luscious and entertaining life.

> *Life Design Journal page 201: List any situation you want to alter. Now, fit the specifics of your I-can't-do-it thinking into the T>W>A>H>C>D pattern. Use this Thought-to-Destiny pattern whenever you catch yourself thinking, saying, or doing anything not inline with the outcome you're pursuing.*

Listen, if the life and business destinies you're experiencing are both satisfying and fulfilling, keep doing what you're doing. But if they aren't, then thoughtfully consider your next step and your next path. There're more options and opportunities than you might imagine.

# Chapter 5

WHICH PATH WILL YOU CHOOSE?

*From My Journal:*

*Throwing off the Comforter of Comfortable.*

It was 5:30 AM. A really, really cold Wisconsin morning; the alarm was ringing and the bedroom was frigid. My nose was ice cold and I remember thinking, "Oh my god, I don't want to do this." I grudgingly crawled out from under the cocoon of my heavy blankets, my body slow and sleepy. When my bare feet hit the floor, I followed my instinct to jump back to bed and burrow under the covers for five more minutes. I felt warm and comfortable.

While I was again snuggled under the covers, within a few minutes that feeling of being warm and comfortable passed. I remember thinking that the comfort and warmth I sought by jumping back into bed was not as satisfying nor did it last very long. What was that about?

I couldn't fully enjoy the comfort because I knew I still had to get up and face the cold room. It was always going to be there until I dealt with it. In the long run, that short-term comfort under the covers caused me more discomfort. I wonder how often I follow my instinct to "jump back under the covers" to hide from a little discomfort and end up regretting it later.

*"One does not discover new lands without consenting to lose sight of the shore for a very long time."*

—André Gide

## This Way or That Way

No matter what's triggering your journey to change, you have a choice to travel one of two distinct paths—the first, the **Path of Least Resistance,** is familiar, well-worn, and you can probably travel it with your eyes half closed. The other, the **Path of Thoughtful Transformation** is unknown and untraveled, but it's the path that, if you stick with it, will lead you to your long-desired destiny.

Look at the behaviors under each of the two paths on the following chart. You'll notice that the behaviors needed to walk the Path of Least Resistance are all meant to deaden feelings, while those needed to travel the Path of Thoughtful Transition are, in contrast, uplifting and expansive.

| Path of Least Resistance | Path of Thoughtful Transformation |
|---|---|
| Avoid the Issue<br>*(Inaction, jump ship, etc.)* | Discover real desires<br>Identify genuine obstacles<br>Choose a new direction |
| Anesthetize the Pain<br>*(Drink, work, food)* | Embrace temporary discomfort<br>Commit to staying the course |
| Again<br>*(Repeat same behaviors)* | |

## *Path of Least Resistance*

The well-worn path that you've habitually—there's that word again—traveled when experiencing a trigger to change is the circular **Path of Least Resistance.** Although it feels as if you're striding forward away from the discomfort, this path eventually leads right back to the point where your journey began. So, why do you keep traveling this same path?

You default to this path to avoid the discomfort, real or imagined, when you anticipate needing to change. Even if what you want is the grandest, most awesome thing in the world, you'll still feel anxious. And whenever you experience anxiety your MO is to seek instant relief. Without thinking—there's that word again—you rush forward towards the **Path of Least Resistance** knowing it offers instant, although probably not permanent, relief. You've been down this path before and you're familiar with the obstacles you'll face. Through the years of traveling this path, you've equipped yourself with pain-numbing behaviors, each offering some degree of instant relief.

## *Pain-Numbing Behaviors:*
### I. Avoid the Issue

You tell yourself it really isn't that bad. Or, you ignore the issue, believing it will go away with time. Or, you might remove yourself from the situation or environment, convinced you won't have a problem if you're not faced with it every day. You'll quit the job you actually enjoy because, once again, you have an irritating co-worker. You'll move to another town because "everyone in this city is snobby." When your partner refuses to talk to you, you'll tell yourself he's just going through a bad few years so you'll wait it out. You'll buy larger clothes because the diet just isn't fast enough.

**II. Anesthetize the Pain**

You fall back on your well-honed, unique, discomfort-numbing "addiction." For a few minutes, hours, or days you blank out your problem and avoid feeling any discomfort. You'll call five friends to kvetch over and over and over, drink more than usual, take long naps, watch hours of mindless TV, clean out cabinets, or work late at night and on weekends. Or, you might have my old addiction—reading a mystery book while eating a bowl of Ju-Jus mixed with Fritos.

**III. Again—Repeat the Old Pattern**

You dress up old behaviors and habits, calling them new and improved, convinced it's going to be different the next time. But, it's just more of the same behavior in a different costume. You'll date a different person from the same office, change jobs but stay in the same line of work, throw more money at yet another management training program, or buy a new house in a city you never really liked to get away from the pesky neighbors.

Whichever pain-avoiding behaviors you use, they will definitely quell your immediate discomfort, but they won't do anything in the long run to get you to your long-desired outcome.

## *Pain-numbing Behavior in Action*
**Repeated Relationship Behavior**

You're ecstatic, sighing with relief and contentment. For the last three months you've been in a great relationship. You know this one is better than all the others! Then he/she dumps you, cheats on you, verbally abuses you, insults your friends, stops calling, or now claims to hate basketball games. God, you've been there before, actually many times before. You feel worthless, angry, frustrated, bored, lonely, and tired, once again. You hate these feelings and you crave relief.

If you travel the **Path of Least Resistance** you might either:
- **Avoid the issue** by saying "I don't care" or "I'm moving to another neighborhood so I won't have to run into him/her."
- **Anesthetize your pain** by eating, calling friends, drinking too much, or watching TV for hours.
- **Again,** you'll say that he/she is a jerk like all the others. You'll get dressed up, call your same friends and again head out to a familiar bar and act the same way. You'll tell yourself that when the next he/she shows up it will be miraculously different. The next one will be the perfect relationship. And, sure enough someone will show up. But what do you want to bet that this relationship will be good for about three months and then the "dumping" will again begin?

Which Path Will You Choose?

## *Repeated Sales Team Behavior*

It's early March and your boss informs you that your sales team finally reached its goal in February. Ever since you took this job nine months ago, directing your team to achieve this goal has been an ongoing struggle. Now, you think, you can finally focus on other department goals. Then in April you find out that your department sales for the month of March were the lowest in company history. Your optimistic outlook and the relief you felt last month shatters. "Damn that sales' team," you think.

If you travel the **Path of Least Resistance** you might:

- **Avoid the issue** by saying, "I can't do any more than I've already done." or "This team is just lazy, I'm going to get another job and let them sink."
- **Anesthetize your pain** by stopping for drinks to commiserate with Adam, who understands because he has the same problems at his new company; or by calling in sick and taking two days off to go fishing; or by shopping for shoes during your lunch hour—a new pair of shoes always makes you feel better.
- **Again** you'll repeat your monthly mantra to the staff that "goals must be met or heads will roll." Or you'll show yet another sales video or enroll "these lunkheads" in one more motivational sales workshop.

> *Life-Design Journal page 205: What pain-avoiding, anesthetizing, or repeating behavior do you use? What's your first action, your first thought, or the first words out of your mouth when you're feeling uncomfortable? What's the first thing you're inclined to do?*

**Avoiding** the issue, **anesthetizing** the pain, and **again** repeating old actions are "behavioral-pain-pills" for discomfort. For a short time you feel better or don't feel at all. The "pills" may temporarily deaden your feelings of hopelessness, guilt, distress or anxiety but, like most other painkillers, there's no long-term, lasting effect. When the numbing effect of those avoiding, anesthetizing, and repeating behaviors wears off—and it will—you'll find yourself back at the beginning of the **Path of Least Resistance** where, once again, you'll be nudged by the same desperate do-something-right-now "trigger" that you've reacted to so many times before.

Once again you'll be staring at the same bottom line, producing the same non-saleable products, dating the same type of guy, weighing the same weight, having the same chaos in your company, or finding yourself thinking that hope, happiness and lasting satisfaction are all illusions and that your dreams will never happen. You'll hear yourself say, "Why isn't this working? Why does this keep happening? Don't they know any better? Why do I always attract people who won't work, who have no loyalty, who are unwilling to do what I tell them? Where are all the good women/men?"

Defaulting to the **Path of Least Resistance,** and medicating yourself with its pain-numbing behaviors will add one more repetitious chapter to your life story that begins with your intention to change and ends with nothing altered except for your self-esteem, which has been knocked down another notch because you wimped out.

Your desired destiny or goal is still "out there." Your happiness is still "out there." Your problem is still not solved nor are you any closer to solving it. The only difference is that you have less self-esteem. Traveling the **Path of Least Resistance** doesn't change one damn thing. It is exhausting, frustrating, and fruitless.

But what other option is there?

*"It is a mistake to look too far ahead. Only one link in the chain of destiny can be handled at a time."*

—Winston Churchill

## *Path of Thoughtful Transformation*

Being forced out from under a "Comforter of Comfort" is how it will feel when you step away from the **Path of Least Resistance,** toss out your pain-numbing habits, and consider traveling another path. If, during that internal dueling of "in or out," "this way or that way," you make a decision not to crawl under the covers of comfort but to venture towards an unexplored direction, your self-esteem will ratchet up ten notches. Once you commit—in that second, that iota of a second—commit to another path, the **Path of Thoughtful**

**Transformation,** you'll be on your way to finally experiencing the life, the career, the retirement, the relationship, or the peace you've always craved.

"Okay Jo Anne. I'll consider taking a different path. BUT, unless the people and circumstances around me change, **I'll** never have a chance at happiness! And **I** really don't like being uncomfortable. Couldn't **I** just could be 'beamed up'?"

### I, I, I

"I" being the operative word here. Your odds are a thousand times greater you'll be "beamed up" than that those people or circumstances you're using as an excuse will turn themselves inside out so you have permission to change. Transformation will only happen if you thoughtfully and purposely make the choice to travel in a new direction using a different path—**Path of Thoughtful Transformation,** a path that leads to a new way of thinking, a new destiny, a new life, new success, new everything.

Will this journey to create life or business changes be faster and easier than your other efforts traveling the **Path of Least Resistance?** Well, that all depends on the meaning you choose to give to each step you take or each challenge you face. Remember this is not a supersonic journey; it's a self-directed walk that you travel at your own pace. Both the **Path of Least Resistance** and the **Path of Thoughtful Transformation** have hills and bends in the road. Both of them will, at times, cause you to sweat and feel uncomfortable. There's no way around it. So you might wonder, "Then why not make it easy on myself and go back to the Path of Least Resistance? I already know the way and it's one less thing I have to think about."

Well, that's true. But let me remind you, it's also the path leading you right back to the destiny you're living in right now. Again, if you are 100% happy with your life and business, then don't make any changes. But, if you aren't happy, then take a new path and make the decision to lighten your "baggage" by dumping all non-serving beliefs or stories you've hauled along on your other failed attempts to change.

The **Path of Thoughtful Transformation** leads to a destiny of your own design. Traveling this path puts the decisions and responsibility for your outcomes in your lap. When you choose this path, you get to decide who and what you'll include or what you'll release. Along this path, instead of being a story re-teller, you'll become the writer and director of a better-ending story.

You can't walk along the **Path of Thoughtful Transformation** with your eyes closed. Unlike the mechanical, habitual steps you took along the **Path of Least Resistance,** each step along the **Path of Thoughtful Transformation** is, well, thoughtful. Once you complete both the internal and external work to prepare for this unique journey, you won't ever have to do it again. When you're ready to focus on other goals and adventures, you'll already have done the work and will know what you want, how you want it, and what you have to do to get it so that you stay on the course to your thoughtful destiny.

> *Life-Design Journal page 206: Reflecting on your level of urgency from page 185, record any thoughts you have about this path taking longer to travel. Also, include any gut reactions to not having your pain-avoiding, anesthetizing, or repeating behaviors to use when you feel uncomfortable.*

"*Okay, Jo Anne, I'm sold. My 'shoes are made for walking' and I am ready to go. Let's get this show on the road!*"

I know you're eager to get going. But remember, you're traveling the **Path of Thoughtful Transformation.** So the first step is a non-step. Just Stop!

# LIBERATION

## Chapter 6

STOP! DON'T DO ANYTHING

From My Journal:

It's Sunday morning and I woke up feeling really good. Had plans to go to the movie at the art museum and then to dinner with Naomi. After showering, I weighed myself. I was up four pounds. "Oh my god!"

Within seconds my distress is unbearable. I called Naomi and made up some lame excuse about not feeling well (and I didn't). Yet again, I let feeling miserable trump having fun. I've got to do something right now. I can't stand feeling like this. So I hop in the car to go buy that diet book I heard about on Oprah. I'm now at the coffee shop; book in hand, hoping to find some promise miracle that will alleviate the distress I feel.

Whew! I've taken a step to solve my problem and suddenly I'm feeling less miserable. The number on the scale hasn't changed since this morning and I haven't taken one damn recommended diet step. But doing something, just anything, makes me feel better.

I've done this many times before. I must have a hundred diet books on my shelf and the numbers on the scale still haven't changed all that much. But that number, whatever it is, still has the power to make me miserable. Why would it be any different this time? It won't! Another diet book isn't going to make one damn bit of difference.

What can I do instead? What do I have to change about myself to get the weight of this weight off my back once and for all?

## *Stop!*

Don't jump, don't leap, don't run, don't skip, hike, or walk. Don't move. Don't do anything.

To "Stop!" is contrary to every habit you adopted when you traveled the Path of Least Resistance. On that path you automatically sprinted forward to "get on with it" or to "fix it ASAP!" By habit you rushed off without thinking. You imagined relief from confusion, pain, dissatisfaction, angst, or fear and hoped you'd finally attain your goal or solve that pain-in-the-butt problem. But the permanent and sustainable relief you were rushing to experience was never on that path, nor was your dream destiny or the answer to your problem. And it never will be.

Each and every business, team, organization or individual I've worked with resists this first **non-step**. Every self-help and business improvement book they've read coached them to take immediate **action:** "Get off your butt! Move forward! Repeat an affirmation! Create a checklist. Stay accountable." After reading the book they were pumped and vowed to follow every morsel of advice. But within a few days or perhaps, if they were persistent, a few weeks, nothing changed and they again felt discouraged and disheartened. Trust me, you won't get the permanent results you want unless you take the time to explore several soul-searching questions:

- What does your ideal destination really look and feel like? If you could have it all, what do you honestly want?
- What beliefs and stories are you going to intentionally carry along with you? Which are you going to leave behind? How will you decide between the two?

- What thoughts, words, and actions do you need to change so you don't keep ending up in the same place with the same destiny?
- What support or tools will you need when you feel lost, confused, discouraged or want to retreat? What will keep you on course until the end?

Until you answer these questions posed in the next few chapters, don't move a muscle, just STOP

> *Life-Design Journal page 207: Stop for a moment to let the work you've done so far settle in. Today, instead of writing in this journal, call a friend to engage in a feeling-good activity. Take a few hours to experience some of the benefits of living a thoughtful, transformed life. What did you do?*

# Chapter 7

## WHAT DO YOU REALLY WANT?

*From My Journal:*

    Last Sunday I put a deposit down on a new house. It was my dream house and I was excited. Everything I ever wanted and more. I wanted to make sure I wasn't kidding myself so I asked Tami to go through the house with a list that I created years ago entitled "My Perfect House:"

- ✓ Three or four bedrooms (so guests would feel comfortable)
- ✓ Large open floor plan (about 3000 sq. ft.)
- ✓ Swimming pool
- ✓ Fireplace
- ✓ Beautifully landscaped yard with lots of trees
- ✓ Two- or three-car garage
- ✓ In a lovely neighborhood conducive for walking
- ✓ Large kitchen area with a long island for entertaining friends
- ✓ Lots of bright light coming in all sides
- ✓ Safe neighborhood with friendly neighbors for get-togethers

    Tami ended up checking off every single item. Plus she added bonus items not on that list: an actual Koi pond with running water (great for meditation), a large, grassy, shaded area that I could use for working outside with clients, and a huge second sitting room where I could facilitate groups for weekly workshops. There were three other buyers waiting to put down escrow money. But I beat them to it. I was going to finally have my dream home.

    It is now Thursday morning. Yesterday I went back to the sellers and said I didn't want the house.

    On Tuesday it hit me that my so-called ideal house was imagined, in part, thirty years ago on that drive with Mom and Dad when I was told that I'd never live in a huge house like the ones we were seeing along Lake Shore Drive. The house I had just put money down on was a house that I imagined the "other people" lived in, and by purchasing it I was going to prove Mom and Dad wrong. I could already hear friends and family say, "You have that dream home. You made it happen."

But what socked me in the gut yesterday was that my dream house was from an old version of who I used to be and how I imagined I'd live my life. At this point in my life I'm single and live alone. I travel all the time. I have overnight visitors a couple of weeks a year. I don't have time for home maintenance or cleaning 3000 sq. ft. of space, most of which I won't use.

What the hell was I thinking?!?! What I thought I wanted is not at all what I want at this point in my life. I'm not that person anymore and that is not my dream house anymore. That dream is truly outdated.

## *What Do You* Really *Want at the End of Your Journey?*

"What do you want?" I asked Jill. "At the end of our time together, what has to change for you to say, 'Wow, this process and our work together was really worth it.'"

Jill has lost sleep, been frustrated, confused, scared, unsure, and speculated about why she feels "out of sync" with her life for years. She's tried time and again to clarify, fix, solve, and change this situation. For some reason, she hasn't found the answers or solutions. She asks for my help and tells me she's committed to investing time, money, and energy to finally get what she's been trying so hard to achieve. I know she's smart, clever, and decisive. So surely she must have ready, well-thought-out answers to the question, "What do you really want?" Nope. Jill, like most other clients, doesn't have a ready answer to that all-important question.

Why don't most people know what they truly want? Simply, it's because their present-day "wants" are clouded by, guess what, their old stories and subconscious beliefs. To clear those clouds there are four probing questions that, when explored and answered, will get you very close to the picture of the life or business destiny you really want, not an outdated, wishful, destiny from a former time in your life.

**Question 1: What Don't You Want?**

Since "pain" has a louder voice than "pleasure" and is screaming in their psyche, clients usually answer, "What do you want?" with a litany of what they **don't want.** So let's start there.

"**I don't want:**
  To be in an office with chaos
  To have a staff that is unmotivated
  To feel old and useless
  To feel out of sync with my life
  To be paralyzed by the economy
  To be treated like this anymore
  To be fat
  To live in such a hot place
  To be alone
  To not have enough money
  To be wary of the future
  To have everyone else get promoted
  To have no time for my family
  To feel guilty."

"Okay," I reply, "If that's what you **don't want,** what **do you** want?"

**Question 2: What Do You "Allegedly" Want?**
After asking that question I'll hear:
  "Oh, I get it:
  - "Since I don't want chaos, I must want order and peace."
  - "Since I don't want a lazy staff, I must want energetic employees."

- "Since I don't want to feel old and useless, I must want to feel young and valuable."
- "Since I don't want him to treat me badly, I must want him to value me."
- "Since I don't want to be fat, I must want to be thin."
- "Since I don't want to be poor, I must want more money."
- "Since I don't want soft sales numbers, I must want to exceed my goal."
- "Since I don't want to be out of sync with life, I must want to feel back in the flow."
- "Since I don't want him to get the promotion, I must want it myself."
- "Since I don't have enough time for my family, I must want more time with them."

"Aha," they'll say, "I get it." But, whatever they say, and however pumped they feel, they're still not ready to jump off the starting block. I'll restrain them with, "Not so fast. For now, let's refer to these as your **Alleged-Do-Wants.**"

Since you're on a conscious, thoughtful journey down an untraveled path to an alleged destiny, are you 100% sure what you want is truly what you want? Are you sure it is not the product of an old story of who you used to be? And let me also ask this, "Is what you say you want today honestly your personal desire? Or have you, by osmosis, adopted it from family aspirations, business dictates, society mores, or advertising edicts?"

## Question 3: Why, Why and Why, Again?

To get to the depth of what you really want, answer one clarifying question: **"Why** do I want to solve, achieve, or create this?" If "want" is the head, "why" is the heart. If "want" is the goal, then "why" is the passion needed to get to that goal. Your answers to **"Why** do I want that?" become the fuel that will sustain you along your untraveled path. Repeatedly asking and answering "why?" will unlock your Pandora's box, which has kept your dreams hidden and the answers to your problems unresolved.

## Importance of "Why?"

After twenty years of coaching, I think I know why clients want what they tell me they want, but I always need to ask "Why?" That one simple question prevents me from making assumptions about their goals based on my story, my beliefs, my experiences, and my personal twist.

**Brad says,** *"I want my manager to be a better leader."*

Without asking "Why?" I might assume he wants his manager to create a clearer vision. But Brad might want to stop the chaos so he can sleep at night.

**Lance and Charlotte say,** *"We want to figure out what we're going to DO when we retire."*

Without asking "Why?" I might assume they want to discuss travel and volunteer options. But instead, they might be concerned about becoming depressed and dying young like Lance's father did.

Running off blindly without asking yourself "Why?" is akin to knowing you want to travel but not knowing where you're going, what to pack, how long you'll be gone, how you're going to pay for it, or what you're going to do when you get there. Remember, the goal of a thoughtful journey is getting to the right place, at the right time, with the right people. Before you expend any energy in any direction, you first need to know exactly where you're going and why you're going there.

But, asking and answering "why" just once isn't enough. Your first response just scratches the surface of your consciousness. But, repeatedly asking "And, why that?" to each of your answers will push you to dig deep to discover your unrealized, unspoken desires. You're digging to discover the one answer that has you light up and say, "Yes, that's it. That's exactly what I want!"

~ ~ ~

## How it Looks in Real Life

**Why + Why + Why = What You Really Want**

Using **alleged-do-wants** from page 83, let's "why" them until we get to "Yes, that's it!"

**Alleged-do-want #1:**

"Since I **don't want** office chaos, I must want order and peace."

"**Why** do you want order and peace?"

"Because the chaos drives me crazy."

## What Do You Really Want?

"**Why** do you want to stop being driven crazy?"
 "Because I can't get my work done during the day."
"**Why** do you want to get your work done during the day?"
 "So I don't go home frazzled and tired."
"**Why** do you want to go home less frazzled and tired?"
 "So I have time to be present for my family."
 "So I have time to work on my boat."
 "So I have the energy to take a dance class."
 "So I can prepare a decent meal and leisurely enjoy it."

Okay, so what you **really want** is to have time to play together with your family, work on your boat, take dance lessons, and prepare and eat leisurely meals?

 *"Yes that's what I want!"*

**Alleged-do-want #2:**
 "Since I **don't want** to be fat, I must want to be thin."
"**Why** do you want to be thin?"
 "So I can fit in my clothes."
"**Why** do you want to fit in your clothes?"
 "So I look better."
"**Why** do you want to look better?"
 "So I'm not embarrassed when I'm in public."
"**Why** don't you want to feel embarrassed in public?"
 "So I can freely enjoy life and my surroundings without any thought of how I look."

Aha, so what you **really want** is to feel comfortable no matter where you are and to finally enjoy your life. Right?

"*Yes that's what I want!*"

**Alleged-do-want #3:**
"Since I **don't want** him to get the promotion, I must want it myself."
"**Why** do you want the promotion?"

"So I can be out from under my supervisor and make more money."

"**Why** do you want to get away from your supervisor?"

"So I can be stress-free when I get home and enjoy my hobbies."

"**Why** do you want more money?"

"So I have more in my savings account."

"**Why** do you want to have a larger savings account?"

"So I can take a trip."

"So I can feel secure."

"**Why** do you want to take a trip?"

"So I can be stimulated by new experiences."

Okay, so what you **really want** is to enjoy your hobbies, feel financially secure, travel, and be exposed to new experiences.

"*Yes that's what I want!*"

∽ ∽ ∽

## Question 4: What Do You Honestly Want?

Now you're at the **heart** of what you truly long for. And it's here, in your heart, where you'll finally get the answer to, "What do I **really want** in my one precious, extraordinary life?"

> I want more time to myself.
> I want to feel engaged in life.
> I want to leave work smiling.
> I want to not work.
> I want to go places.
> I want to share your love.
> I want to play more.
> I want to make a contribution.
> I want my life to mean something.
> I want to leave a legacy.
> I want to feel good about myself.
> I want to quit hiding from life.
> I want to write, paint, sculpt, dance, sing, hike, bike, canoe, fish, and make love.

Once you get to this level of articulated, heartfelt clarity, you can't and won't want to stop. Your for-real, honest-to-God, tell-it-like-it-is internal voice is tired of not being heard. It's tired of nudging, coaxing, prodding, and screaming at you to finally listen to the one or two or three REAL things you want.

Living Your 'Someday' Now

"NO, I don't just want another boyfriend;
I WANT TO BE RESPECTED."

"NO, I don't want another employee policy;
I WANT TO GO SAILING."
"NO, I don't want another job;
I WANT TO LOVE WHAT I AM DOING."

"NO, I don't want to get over my malaise;
I WANT TO FEEL PASSIONATE AGAIN."

"NO I don't want another diet;
I WANT TO WALK THE BEACH."

Finally, you're listening to your inner voice, your heart, and your deepest wants. Now you know where you're heading and why you're going that way. Now, you're consciously aware of the true nature of what your spirit craves and what it will suffer if you stop your journey or stray off the path.

> *Life-Design Journal page 208: To get to the truth of what your heart, mind, and soul really want and to liberate your "Aha's," answer the four Destiny-Clarifying questions:*
> *What don't you want?*
> *What do you allegedly want?*
> *Why do you want what you want?*
> *What do you really, really want?*

## *Now What?*

Since you have clarity about what you really want, when are you going to take your first steps towards your new life? The next two to three months? The next six months? One year? Five years? Never? Why not right now?

# Chapter 8

WHY DON'T YOU ALREADY HAVE
WHAT YOU WANT?

*From My Journal:*

During one of the timeouts last night at the Suns' game, a fan had an opportunity to earn money by shooting free throws. MADD and an Anti-Drinking task force sponsored this event. The fan was told he'd get $25 for every free throw he made. This extremely tall man had obviously played basketball before because he was hitting free throws as the announcer was talking. You could almost see him counting his prize money.

But, before the clock was set for the allotted thirty seconds, the announcer told him he had to wear a pair of glasses that replicated how he would see things if he were 1 ½ times over the limit for drunk driving.

In the next thirty seconds he attempted shot after shot. He missed the backboard completely with the first shot; the next was two feet off to the left, then one was three feet to the right. He got so frustrated he stood directly under the basket and threw the ball—that time it went over the top. Didn't hit the target once. Didn't make any money.

When he took off the glasses you could see his frustration. He knew how to shoot baskets, did it time and again, but when his perception was skewed, no matter how often he tried or from what vantage point, he missed the target.

That's just what I do when I see things through my limiting beliefs and perceptions. I keep missing the target.

## *Why Not Now?*

*"Jo Anne, I understand everything you're saying and I really want to change, but I can't do it right now because...."*

Wait a minute. You know what you really want, and you have a pretty good idea of all that you'll give up if you don't complete your journey. So why don't you just go out and get what you want—at this moment? It's not for lack of desire or that you're a lazy lout or commitment phobic. For God's sake, in the past you've set and reached hundreds of goals. When the going got tough, you sucked it up and pushed forward every day. So why are you hesitating to address this challenge or achieve this goal? Why are you still settling for a "less-than-ideal life?" Have you convinced yourself that living an 80% life is all you can possibly ask for? Do you only think of "happily ever after" as a fairy tale? Don't know what it is?

Actually, the answer is quite simple.

Your beliefs, both obvious and hidden, are preventing you from becoming the person who's ready and able to take the first step. To understand what those beliefs are, complete this simple sentence: "I want to BUT..." Then from that answer, extrapolate the beliefs holding you hostage.

꩜ ꩜ ꩜

**Let me show you what I mean:**

I'll again ask the question: "If you know what you **really want**, why don't you already have it?"

## I. Statements:

I **really want** to feel passionate, BUT I'm sixty-five and too old to feel passionate.

I **really want** a new career, BUT only young kids are getting hired these days.

I **really want** to go sailing, BUT I can't afford a sailboat.

I **really want** to stop obsessing about my weight, BUT to do that I'll need a stomach staple.

I **really want** to have a loving man in my life, BUT men only like much younger women.

I **really want** to have a loving woman in my life, BUT women only like rich men.

I **really want** to travel to Greece, BUT I have no one to travel with.

I **really want** to buy a boat, BUT in this economy it's impossible.

I **really want** to feel less stress, BUT employees today are irresponsible and lazy.

## II. Limiting Beliefs:

So let me get this straight. What you're really saying is that you **believe** that:

- Sixty-five is too old to feel passion.
- Only young kids get hired.
- You have to buy a sailboat in order to go sailing.

- Only a stomach staple will stop the voices in your head.
- All men are shallow and prefer younger women.
- Women are only interested in men with thick wallets.
- The only way to go to Greece is if a friend comes along.
- Businesses are never profitable in an economy like this.
- All employees are irresponsible, lazy, and don't know how to work.

*Really?*

Here's the reality. You won't feel passion, not because you're sixty-five, but because **you believe** being sixty-five turns off the passion dial. You won't increase company profits, not because the economy sucks, but because **you believe** the media sources telling you it will be at least five years before you can expect any business growth. You won't find an amazing partner, not because you're not rich or don't have a model's body, but because **you believe** everyone in the whole wide world values wealth and good looks above everything else.

### COACHING NOTE:

*Put the following statement on your screen saver or, better yet, memorize it, "My beliefs are not unchangeable, absolute truths. Once I own them, I give them meaning and create false parameters about whether or not I'll be able to do what I want. Through my thoughts, words, and subsequent actions I created the destiny I'm living right now. But I can change that destiny in this next moment."*

*Life-Design Journal page 212: For each of your answers to "What do you really want?" on page 211 extrapolate the limiting belief that's keeping you stuck.*

# Chapter 9

## METAPHORICALLY *"LOBOTOMIZE"* LIMITING BELIEFS

*From My Journal:*

During Easter brunch Robin said, "Where's my signed copy of that book that you promised me last year?"

I grabbed a mimosa and said, "Now that e-readers are the rage, I'm not sure if a book like mine would work as an e-book. I first need to do some research on that. And then I need to hire an editor, a page designer and a cover artist and I'm a bit short on expendable funds. So I need to hold off for now."

He didn't say anything. Then three days ago he called and asked if we could meet for coffee.

I assumed it was to chat. But when he got to the coffee shop, he nailed me and said, "Listen, if you don't want to finish the book, okay don't finish it. No one will think anything less of you. But for two years now you've talked about the book. For ten years your clients have achieved incredible results. NOW you're telling me that e-readers and money are the reasons you can't finish. When are you going to quit using excuses? Either finish the book or don't.

And then he continued, "Jo Anne, I'll bet lots of authors have formatted books like yours for e-readers. And if it's money, I'll help you."

I stammered, "Thanks but I can't let you give me money. I wouldn't feel comfortable unless I paid you back with interest and I am not sure when I could do that."

He said, "Now you have another excuse, don't you?" BAM! He used my own "stuff" and nailed me right between the eyes.

In order to finish this book, I've got to metaphorically "Lobotomize" my own procrastinating-producing beliefs that e-books are impossible to format, that formatting is really the problem, and, most revealing, that, yet again, I won't let someone support or help me.

## *Metaphorical "Lobotomy"*

"With a metaphorical lobotomy." I answered when Glenn Swain, my creative writer friend asked me how clients release limiting beliefs. "Great description." he replied. So did the next six people I shared this with. But number seven said, "Oh my god that's awful. I'd never read a book that used that term. 'Lobotomy' is such an awful word." I understood her gut reaction to that word. In the past the word "lobotomy" had a one-dimensional, highly charged, negative meaning. But as super-coach Vickie Champion says, "Nothing has meaning until **you** give it meaning."

For some reason I was digging my heels in on the words "Metaphorical Lobotomy." They seemed the perfect explanation of what needed to occur for someone to imagine life outside of the boundaries of their current "sandbox." So I called Mark Le Doux, an accomplished playwright and a soul mate, to help me make the decision of whether to go with my gut or with conventional beliefs. Mark suggested switching to the word "amnesia." We kicked that idea around for a while and then, playing devil's advocate, Mark asked me why I was reluctant to use the word amnesia. I told him that to me "amnesia" means temporarily forgetting rather than eliminating; to me it means something happening to us with no personal control over the result; to me it means that, although it's unconscious, it's still there waiting to make itself known. And most significantly, to me it means stuffing, ignoring, and a constant battle to keep it under wraps. To me, unlike "amnesia," the word "lobotomy" means making a personal decision to become empowered.

And so I deliberately choose to give "Metaphorical Lobotomy" the meaning that it's a **well-thought-out, personal decision to permanently release a non-serving story, belief, or personal truth that keeps you from experiencing the life you desire.**

"Lobotomy," as I'm using the word, is a concept that suggests that you have control over what influences your life and business. It illuminates and releases as opposed to darkening and imprisoning. It implies that your personal stories and truths can be changed, adjusted, expanded, or redesigned.

"Lobotomize it!" is a tongue-in-cheek declaration to remind yourself that you can stop the insanity of ugly thoughts, judgment, guilt, unattainable dreams, and lost opportunities. At the same time, it's a mental command switch that stops you in your tracks and prevents you from going back to the Path of Least Resistance where, although it's easy, you take no control of or responsibility for your thoughts and feelings.

Mentally shouting "Lobot it!" dissolves the rush of negative energy trying to stop potential joy or adventure. The words "Lobot it!" shock you awake and prevent you from reverting to hardwired limitations keeping you stuck in a rut. Used consciously and repeatedly, "Lobotomizing" unsavory beliefs or behaviors weakens the old neural hardwiring forcing you to live by default and habit. As the old hardwiring, is weakened, new life-supporting wiring begins to solidify, opening the door for you to perceive and interpret options in a new light.

## Metaphorically "Lobotomize" Limiting Beliefs

*"Jo Anne, no matter what word you use, shifting through my beliefs in order to liberate myself from those I don't want sounds time consuming and sort of woo-wooish. Isn't there something else I can do that's easier and faster?"*

Look, you've spent hours, days, and years talking to co-workers, spouses, girlfriends, workout friends, strangers on a plane, and people in coffee shops. You tell yourself, and everyone who will listen, what you want more of or, more likely, what you want to dump out of your life. You enthusiastically paint a picture of your "Someday-Ideal Life" when you'll have the grandest job, smartest employees, largest profits, healthiest body, the best retirement, when you'll climb that mountain, open that African import shop, and travel to Istanbul. Each retelling of your Someday- Ideal-Life story sparks hope and excitement. In that moment the world is a banquet of possibilities. You just know that the day your dreamed-about life becomes actualized, your business, personal life, relationships, and body will be finally be perfect.

Then one day you're struck by the fact that the only operative word in your oft-told story is the word "Someday"— implying that it's still "out there." It suddenly dawns on you: "It just ain't gonna happen, is it? It's all just a fantasy."

So the next time your friend John says, "How's your African import shop project coming along?" you revise the ending of your Someday-Ideal-Life story to say, "My father-in-law just moved in so that's going to take up my time." Or, "With the economy in such terrible shape, it wasn't a good time to leave my 'sucky' job." Or, "Brandon, my partner, decided he wanted to move in a different direction. Now I'm just too old to go it on my own." Once again you've pushed your Someday-Ideal-Life dream to a back burner. You occasionally bring it up—but with a lot less passion and energy. Eventually even friends stop asking about it because they, too, believe it's only a "Someday" wish.

So let me answer your question, "Isn't there something else I can do that would be easier and faster?" with these questions: "Exactly how long have you been telling that same someday-story and how much closer are you today to it being a reality? What makes you believe this metaphoric lobotomy technique isn't easier and faster? Could it be that you're looking at it with a skewed perception?" What if you consciously and intentionally removed your misperception-glasses, i.e., the limitations of your ability to adapt? Might your destination become more visible and your path more travelable?

"Oh come on, Jo Anne, taking off a pair of glasses is easy and immediate. How do I extract and lobotomize an unconscious, hardwired belief that I've owned for twenty years?"

Guess what? I've got an answer to that, too. You do it thoughtfully and deliberately, and you stick with it.

## How to Rid Yourself of Defeating Beliefs
### First Action: Use *"Lobotomize it!"* as a Momentum-Stopper

Before you actually begin shedding obstructive beliefs, equip yourself with some at-the-ready word or phrase that snaps you

## Metaphorically "Lobotomize" Limiting Beliefs

back into focus when your hardwired story of "This is just too much and I'll never get what I want" takes over. Mentally shouting "Lobotomize it!" or any other attention-grabbing phrase shocks you consciously awake. It buys time to refocus, realign, and reroute yourself in the direction of your envisioned destiny. It stops the flow of fear-based messages falsely telling you it's not possible to live your dreams.

> "Oh, I'm just too old to go dancing."
> **Lobotomize it!**
> "I'll never get another well-paying job."
> **Lobotomize it!**
> "There's just no money to hire more people."
> **Lobotomize it!**

**Second Action: "Lobotomize" Three Common Destiny-Diverting Beliefs**

Once you've chosen the word or phrase you'll use to stop imagined or actual discomfort from pushing you off course, the next step is to tackle three commonly held, usually unconscious, beliefs that divert you from forward movement.

### DESTINY-DIVERTING BELIEF #1

"Lobotomize" the belief that your life or business is set in concrete, that you are just who you are, and that you have no choice but to just suck it up.

I can't repeat it often enough: 99% of everything you believe to be absolutely, universally true just isn't. Your beliefs are uniquely yours, so you're the one who can make a conscious choice to "lobotomize" those that aren't in concert with your new life vision. It's not absolutely true that you are just who you are, or that your life and business are set in concrete. If that were your truth, you would never have cooked in a microwave, talked on a cellphone, used a computer, driven a car, finished school, or danced the Funky Chicken.

> *Life-Design Journal page 213: What do you believe is unchangeable or insurmountable in your life, in regards to another person, or concerning a specific situation?*

### DESTINY-DIVERTING BELIEF #2

"Lobotomize" the belief that all life or business changes are going to be painful, arduous, will never truly happen, and are flat out no fun.

Take a moment to remember those times when this wasn't true: You learned how to ski, ride a bike, and drive a car. How about the time you got a new haircut and loved it, or when you started a new career and excelled at it? There's no way you would've gotten this far in life if you hadn't faced new challenges, practiced, made a few mistakes, and then finally became skilled at what you were trying to learn or change.

## Metaphorically "Lobotomize" Limiting Beliefs

Sure, some changes and learning experiences may have been unpleasant. But you've got to admit, a lot of them were fun and easy, too. Either way, you changed. If you choose to hang on to the change-is-painful belief and totally ignore the times it wasn't, you're making a **choice** to stay stuck right where you are.

> *Life-Design Journal page 214: List at least five times you've made changes or learned new skills that were enjoyable experiences. When you're tempted to go down the "I hate changing and I'm going to stop now" spiral, you can refer back to these experiences to break that old untrue thought pattern.*

### DESTINY-DIVERTING BELIEF #3
#### A huge one!

"Lobotomize" the belief that it's more virtuous to have a less-than life than a wonderful life.

You don't help someone who's poor by being poor yourself, or someone who's unhappy by remaining miserable, or someone who's sick by declaring your ailing health. There's not a finite amount of goodness, or greatness, or happiness for everyone to share. What you experience or enjoy is not coming from someone else's account. Everything you need or want is in your personal, unlimited abundance account waiting for you to make a withdrawal. It's only through your bigness that you'll have the ability and strength to help others. It's only through your happiness and sense of contentment that others will be drawn to you. When you're the biggest and best you can be, you become a model for others to become their biggest and best selves.

> *Life-Design Journal page 214: Write about a time when you downplayed feeling joyful or when you minimized a successful business outcome because you thought if you made yourself seem "less than" or "not okay" it would make someone else feel better.*

Now that you've liberated yourself from the beliefs that you're an immovable, concrete being; that change is fraught with pain; and that it's not okay to have it all; and, now that you know how to stop the run-amok poisonous thoughts tempting you to swerve off course, let's look at how you can uncover and liberate yourself from the specific beliefs preventing you from living your best life.

**Uncover, Lobotomize, and Upgrade Your Personal Beliefs**

For more than twenty-five years, I've observed clients struggling to excavate the beliefs, opinions, and attitudes keeping them stranded in place. To make this process easier, I developed a five-step template that uncovers both conscious and unconscious beliefs.

## Metaphorically "Lobotomize" Limiting Beliefs

> *What do you want:* _____
> 1. State why you don't already have what you want.
> 2. List your beliefs based on the statements you just made.
> 3. Declare those beliefs "lobotomized" and replace them with empowering beliefs.
> 4. If you "owned" those new empowering beliefs, what would you think, say, and do (T>W>A) differently?
> 5. If you're resistant to taking any of those actions or adopting the new empowering beliefs, start over with #1.

By using these five steps, you'll uncover unacknowledged beliefs and pinpoint the specific thoughts and words that keep you running in the same repetitive loop. With practice you'll become quite adept at supplanting these beliefs, thoughts, and words with others that support, rather than thwart, your forward movement.

Let me show you how it works with two examples—one personal and one career.

✥ ✥ ✥

### PERSONAL ILLUSTRATION:

**The want:** *"I really want to dress with flair and be spontaneously engaged with life."*

**1. State why you don't already have what you want.**

"That's a lovely idea, but I'm fifty-three and at this age women should be appropriately dressed and not dressed like some thirty-something tart. Besides, my friends will gossip and say I'm losing it."

2. **List your beliefs based on that statement.**
    - "Being fifty-three has inherent limits.
    - "I know exactly what all my friends think.
    - "If they did think I was goofy, I'd let their thoughts trump my happiness."

3. **Declare those beliefs lobotomized and replace them with empowering beliefs.**
    "I'm at the stage of life where I have no restrictions. I owe it to myself to have as much fun and be as happy as I can. My friends get such a kick out of the new me."

4. **If you "owned" those new beliefs, what you would think, say and do differently?**
    - "I'd stop **thinking** that at fifty-three my life is on the downhill slide and there are inherent limits connected to my age.
    - "I'd stop using the **words,** 'It's a bitch to get old' or 'I'm glad I'm not young anymore.' Instead I'd say, 'This is really a great time of my life.'"
    - "I'd **buy** a funky blouse, tie a colorful scarf around my neck, take a walk along the beach, skip stones in the water, and say 'hey' to everyone I meet."

## Metaphorically "Lobotomize" Limiting Beliefs

**5. If you're resistant to taking any of those actions or adopting those new empowering beliefs, start over with # 1.**

*Starting over:*
**1. State why you don't already have what you want.**

"That sounds like fun but I don't have time right now to buy a new blouse, and besides, there's no way I can opt out of morning coffee with my husband's family so I can take the 'new' me for a walk on the beach."

**2. List your beliefs based on those answers.**
- "It takes a lot of time to buy a blouse.
- "I can only walk on the beach in the morning.
- "My in-laws are inflexible and won't let me miss morning coffee."

**3. Declare those beliefs lobotomized and replace them with empowering beliefs.**

"I have all the time, energy, and support I need to be happy. It's such fun to be me. Everyone loves the new me."

**4. If you "owned" those new beliefs, what you would think, say and do differently?**
- "I'd buy a couple of new blouses and when I'm strolling through town later I'll look for some great scarves to match.

- "I'm going to **say,** 'I'm getting a new and improved lease on my life. Do you want to go for a walk with me?'"
- "I'm going to quit **thinking** that my in-laws and other people are incapable of changing or, more honestly, have control over my ability to change."

**5. If you're resistant to taking any of those actions or adopting the new empowering beliefs, start over with # 1.**

CAREER ILLUSTRATION:

**The Want:** *"I've always wanted to be an event planner."*

**1. State why you don't already have what you want.**
- "Because to be a successful event planner, I'll have to interact with wealthy people and I am far too shy to do that (**Beliefs**).
- I don't fit in with those people (**Thoughts**).
- They have lots of money, are dressed better, or have advanced degrees, and I wouldn't know what to say to them (**Beliefs and Words**).
- When I'm in group situations I either withdraw to a corner, stroll the perimeter of the room, stand near the buffet table and eat myself silly, or spend time powdering my nose in the restroom (**Actions**)."

## Metaphorically "Lobotomize" Limiting Beliefs

2. **List your beliefs based on those answers.**
   - "I believe the only way to be a successful event planner is to interact with wealthy people at fancy-schmantzy events and mixers."
   - "I believe only wealthy people need event planners."
   - "I believe I'm shy around people with money."
   - "I believe I must have a degree to be able to talk to potential customers."
   - "I believe the only safe places at an event are in a corner, at the buffet table, or talking to another 'lost soul.'"

3. **Declare those beliefs lobotomized and replace them with empowering beliefs.**

   "I'm a sought-after event planner. My skills are unique and highly appreciated. The people in this room may know how to go to a party but they don't know how to create a party. I do! Everyone I meet, whether wealthy or not, has the need for an event planner or knows someone who does. I'm exactly what they're looking for."

4. **If you "owned" those new beliefs, what you would think, say and do differently?**

   "I'm going to dress in a creative way **(new action)** and look forward to meeting someone interesting **(new thoughts)**. I'll walk in with confidence, and approach someone who seems interesting. I'll introduce myself and ask her questions about herself. When asked what I do, I'd say with confidence, 'I'm an event planner who specializes in creating memories.'" **(new words)**.

**5. If you're resistant to taking any of those actions or adopting the new empowering beliefs, start over with # 1.**

> *Life-Design Journal page 215: Practice this exercise by stating one thing you've always wanted or one thing you'll regret not experiencing. Take time as you go through each step. Pay close attention to the words, thoughts, and actions you're using to rationalize why you don't already have what you want. Then, be equally thoughtful about replacing them with alternatives that are empowering and supportive.*

Listen, I'm not suggesting you change everything in your life right now. As I've said before, you tried that and it didn't work. This transformational journey is paced and thoughtful, but it's always forward moving. Start by taking small steps: Change a thought or a word, or incorporate a new action in your life. Perhaps your first step will be to walk in a department store and, for the first time, look at clothes that have "flair," holding them in front of you as you look in the mirror. The next time you might actually try a few on. If you're the shy event planner, maybe take that first small step by introducing yourself to the barista at the coffee shop. Or, perhaps attend a lecture you believe

## Metaphorically "Lobotomize" Limiting Beliefs

is "over your head" and introduce yourself to the person sitting next to you who may, or may not, know more about the topic than you do. Any conversation outside of your comfort zone will increase your confidence in your ability to approach potential customers.

Whatever you choose, repeat it until it becomes habit, feels natural, and becomes the new "you." With each step you'll overcome challenges and find yourself closer to your goal. This time it won't be an idle dream or wishful thinking. This time, because you did the work and stayed with it, you'll finally be living a new story that has a satisfying ending, day after day after day.

# CREATION

# Chapter 10

## WHAT ELSE IS ON YOUR BUCKET LIST?

From My Journal:

When did my first Life-Defining Play close?
I'd been teaching for ten years and was twenty-eight when I quit, packed my Suburban, and hit the road. I had no destination in mind. My plan was that when given the choice of two roads, I would take the road that had the least amount of traffic. For nine months I slept on logging roads, in the parking lots of hotels, and in municipal parking lots where the local police promised to keep an eye on me to make sure I was safe.
After my time on the road, I tried teaching for a half-year. It still wasn't right. Next, I took jobs working for the County, got a real estate broker license, worked for a consulting firm, became the executive director of a placement organization, a director of franchise expansions, regional manager of a moving company, VP of recreation for a hotel operation, and a sales VP for an international firm.
I took each of those jobs by default. Either I quit a job out of frustration and felt forced to take the next job that came up, or someone offered me an interesting position and I took it because I was bored and needed something new in my life.
Then the time came when I was bored with my career yet again. I was tired of marking time and didn't want just another job. My "trigger" came one night when I was sleeping and needed to use the bathroom. Since I traveled and stayed in a different hotel each night, when I woke with the urge to "go," I never knew what side of the bed to get out on to use the bathroom. I was aggravated. When I opened my eyes to get my bearings, I was at home in my own bed. That was the moment I knew I had to get another job.
I wanted a new job, but I also thought it was time to work backwards to figure out what it should be. I knew I didn't want any of the careers I had until then. And even though I loved to

travel, I didn't want the leftover home and social life that comes with constant traveling for work. I really had no idea what an idealized life and career looked like for me.

So I asked myself what I **didn't want**:
- ✓ Restrictions on my time, my earning potential, and my opportunities to play and travel
- ✓ For damn sure, I didn't want to sell anything
- ✓ Oh yeah, and I didn't want a boss either
- ✓ I didn't want to be made to stay in one place
- ✓ I didn't want to sit at a desk all day long
- ✓ I didn't want to work with things; I wanted to work with people
- ✓ I hated quotas
- ✓ I didn't want to miss social events because I might not be in town.

If that's true, what does that tell me about what I **want**?
- ✓ Freedom, freedom, freedom
- ✓ To be my own boss
- ✓ To work with people
- ✓ To have the flexibility to work from anywhere
- ✓ To go to social and cultural events
- ✓ To make as much, or as little, as I wanted
- ✓ To have lots of time to explore, however I choose to define that

**Why** do I want those things?
- ✓ I love serendipitous adventures
- ✓ I love nudging others toward their dreams
- ✓ I love traveling to international cities to learn about the people and their culture

- ✓ I love to "see" people as who they are and not as who I expect them to be
- ✓ I love to teach
- ✓ I love to explore and explode the limits of my personal boundaries.

What it all boils down to is that I want a job that supports my life and not a life that supports my job. I don't want to have to pick and choose from the list of things I love. I want it all. It feels "perfect." It feels ideal. So, **I want it all!**

# What Else is on Your Bucket List?

*"The world will not fall apart if we let ourselves express our vastness. It is more likely the world will stop falling apart if we do."*
—*Nelson Mandela*

## *What Is Your "I Want It All?"*

What does your I-have-it-all, ideal life look like? What have you hidden or permanently put on the back burner as superfluous when you've thought of how you'd like to live your life?

"Ideal Life? Jo Anne, I didn't ask for an extreme makeover of my life. I just wanted an answer to my ongoing pain-in-the-butt situation. Besides, there is no such thing as an ideal life."

"Oh really! And why not?"

Yes, you want to increase company profits so you don't lose your job. Of course you want retirement with your spouse to be more of a treat and less of a travesty. Sure you want to lose thirty pounds because your clothes don't fit. Yeah, you want to live near the mountains with the love of your life. But what else do you want?

In the past, when you urgently needed to make a change you put all your focus on that one "not quite right" area of your life. And by habit, (again the habit thing), you put the rest of your life on hold until you "fixed" that damn problem. You examined and re-examined your issue a hundred times. The more you focused on it, the larger its importance became, to the exclusion of every other area of your life.

In total contrast, the Thoughtful Transformation Journey has an everything-is-included perspective. It's about so much more than the fact that you want the office chaos to stop or you want to shed fifteen pounds. It's really about having a satisfying, rewarding life in every **area.**

If you stop the chaos in the office so you can "play together with your family, work on your boat, and prepare and eat leisurely meals:"

- Your health will improve because you're not stressed and you're eating better.
- Your relationship with your family will benefit because you're home more.
- Your leisure time will be enhanced as you finish the boat and go sailing.
- Your knowledge will increase as you learn to cook Chinese.

And slowly as a "Thoughtful Transformation Traveler" you'll not only make the desired changes that triggered the start of your journey, but you'll also be molding a sort of Ideal Destiny—a composite of everything you truly want. So, for now, to use the Thoughts>Words>Actions>Habits>Character>Destiny formula from Chapter 4, let's agree to think of your I-have-it-all-life as an **Ideal Destiny.**

## *Your Ideal Destiny*

To create a visual of your Ideal Destiny, think of it as a jigsaw puzzle. There will be a puzzle piece depicting your health, one depicting your relationships, and another your life purpose. Then there's a career piece, an environment piece, and somewhere under the jumble of pieces is the money or finance piece. Once you unscramble and interlock these pieces, you'll have a portrait of your Ideal Destiny.

The design of each piece will become increasingly apparent as you answer and expand on the questions in each of the following categories. If you have difficulty starting, revisit your notes from page 182, where you listed the various life and business areas that you wanted to see altered. What if you could craft the perfect change in each area? What would that look and feel like?

> *Life-Design Journal page 218: As you read each of the eleven sections below, use the questions posed to create a first draft of what your "Ideal Destiny" might look like if you had it all. Sit with your idealized destiny for a few days. Then return to these pages and re-examine your answers. Add to, delete, or edit as you gain new insight.*

**1. Leisure:**

What would you do with your leisure time if you had all the time, money, health, and energy to make it happen? Do you like to travel? How often would you like to travel? Where? What other recreation would you like to have time for? Do you read, work out, watch TV, or spend time on a hobby? Do you play with your children and grandchildren, solve crossword puzzles, or restore cars? Paint, write, make a movie, dance, roller skate, or climb mountains? How much alone time or down time do you crave?

**2. Education/Learning:**

What would you like to learn? Do you want to earn a specific degree or just take classes on a variety of topics? How do you learn best—by doing, by having a mentor, by reading, by going to school, or by attending workshops?

Would you be interested in traveling somewhere to take classes or to combine learning with some sort of community engagement?

**3. Lifestyle:**

Would you like to cook every day or eat out? How would you like to dress? Do you want to drive or use public transportation? Do you want to eat organically or do you thoroughly enjoy fast foods? Do you like to hang out with close family and friends or do you like to meet new people all the time? Do you want to simplify your life or expand it in any way?

**4. Geography/Environment:**

Where would you like to live? City or country? Small or large community? Do you want to live in more than one place? What size house, apartment, cabin, or RV? Ocean, woods, high desert? Arts, culture, fishing, hunting availability?

**5. Civic Engagement/Volunteer:**

Do you want to volunteer? Do you want to be a leader or a worker? What cause or organization are you most interested in?

How much time do you want to spend? Is there a community or national issue in which you'd like to make a difference?

**6. Career:**

Do you want a career or a job? What might it be? How much do you want to work? What time of the day do you want to engage in this activity? What does your work environment look like? Office, home, coffee shop? Who's part of your workday? How much free time do you want? Do you like being your own boss with no micro-management or are you more comfortable with being given specific directions and told how to do the work?

**7. Health and Wellness:**

What does your physical, emotional, and mental health look like? What are you willing to do to make that happen? Do you want to go to the gym? Walk? Meditate? Read? Nap? How often do you laugh? How often do you want to get hugged and told you are loved? How long do you want to live?

**8. Identity:**

What does your self-esteem look like in this idyllic destiny? Do you want to change it in any way? What do you say about yourself? What do others say about you? What do you love about yourself and how do you live it?

**9. Life's Purpose:**

Where does spirituality or religion fit into your life? How often do you practice, pray, meet, or contemplate each day or week? Do you need or have a sense of purpose? A life mission? Is it important to you to leave a legacy?

**10. Relationships:**

Spouse/partner: Describe that person if you want one. Children: How many? Grandchildren: How involved do you want to be? Extended family: How often do you see them? In what setting? Friends: old friends, new friends? What type of interaction do you want with them? Neighbors: How close? What kind? Old or young? Just exchange over-the-fence greetings or have them over for dinner? Working relationships: Do you want to be social with co-workers or more isolated?

**11. Money/Abundance:**

What do you see in your checking, saving, and retirement accounts? How easily does what you need come to you? Does it always come in the form of money? Do you trade services or time? Do you believe in passing it forward as a philosophy to support yourself? What is your new idealized relationship with money?

Now that you've painted a vibrant picture of your desired future, how can you think of defaulting back to the Path of Least Resistance? And if that picture is not enough to keep you steadily walking forward, consider what you'll be giving up if you don't stay on course and travel your path to its end.

## *Benefits of Living in an Ideal-Destiny*

At a recent retreat, Ellen, an executive from Pennsylvania, returned from a working break with the following list of what she'd be giving up if she didn't stay on her thoughtful transition journey to its end.

"If I give up the **me** I know I want to be and the life I want to live, I give up the following:"

| | |
|---|---|
| Energy | Beautiful restful house |
| Peace | Fun and adventure |
| Rest | Making healthy meals |
| Organization | A nice body |
| Money | Trips with friends |
| Serenity | Winter getaway |
| Health | Time to volunteer |
| My yearnings | Taking Mom to Alaska |
| Meet new people | Dancing |
| A loving mate | Fresh flowers in my house |
| Travel | Nice writing pen |
| House in the woods | Cuddling in bed |
| Walk in Paris | My own opinion |
| Hike in Switzerland | Greater sense of self |
| Coffee in Russia | Financial security |
| Massages | Time to appreciate nature |

| | |
|---|---|
| Inner peace | Slow Sunday mornings |
| Taking friends to dinner | Creativity |
| Having self-confidence | Living in a walkable community |

Ellen's written list is her visual reminder of "why" she's taking this journey. It becomes her passion-pushing fuel. Kept accessible and used, it's her go-to butt-kicker to refocus when she's tired, had a bad day, or tempted to venture off course. When Ellen reads her list, it emotionally and physiologically pulls her focus away from her desire to quit and puts it back on her all-encompassing larger life. She can also redirect and energize her focus by incorporating one small item or activity from her "What I'll Give Up" list into her day: Put flowers in her house, eat a healthy meal, get a massage, dance to music on her iPod, take a walk in a park, call a good friend to join her for dinner. Taking any small action when she feels doubt or discomfort will keep her moving forward to her ideally designed life.

> *Life-Design Journal page 229: Extrapolate the benefits of living your Ideal Destiny by finishing this sentence: "If I give up the **me** I know I want to be and the life I want to live, I give up the following..." You'll refer back to this list later when you create a plan for the support you'll need as you continue on your journey.*

Now that you know what you ideally want, and now that you know what's in the way of achieving it, and now that you know

## What Else is on Your Bucket List?

how to upgrade your thoughts and actions so they're in sync with who you're becoming, you'll collate this knowledge into a new story that will become the passion-sustaining fuel to keep you walking forward. This new story will include everything you want, everyone you want to be with, everywhere you want to go and every feeling you want to experience. It will replace your I-still-don't-have-what-want story and will become the new narrative you'll repeat to yourself and others.

# Chapter 11

## WRITE AN EMPOWERING STORY

*From My Journal:*

Damn it. My gut hurts; I feel anxious and scared. I didn't get that $3,000 city contract. Where the hell are these feelings coming from? I'm picturing myself on the streets and begging for food. It's all crap. But god, it feels like life or death.

Why am I having this reaction to a simple, "Not this time?"

I see it all so clearly. I must have been eight and was sitting with Dad at the kitchen table while he paid bills. He had white envelopes around him. One marked electric, one mortgage, one phone, food, coal, car insurance, doctors, or gas. Then he'd put down a small pile of dollar bills from his cashed factory check.

He took a breath, pulled out a five-dollar bill from the stack and put it into the "electric"-marked envelope. Five dollars was that week's contribution for the monthly electric bill. He continued putting money in each envelope. But the stack of dollars always ran out before all the envelopes were filled.

Then he'd begin the money shuffle. From one envelope to the next he reassigned the dollars. Which bill was due first? Which envelope could he borrow from before that bill was due? He worked two, sometimes three, jobs. Yet, there was never enough to fill all the envelopes. It was always a juggling act. From electric to gas, from car insurance to food.

After seeing him worry week after week, I stuffed my wants and I stuffed my fears. Oh no, there was no way I was going to be responsible for any more of his stress. I decided that if I couldn't earn it myself, I wouldn't want it. I think that's when I began to live the story of a girl who worked really hard to get whatever she needed... not what she wanted. I never asked for help or for things. I never again wanted to feel as if what I wanted put pressure on someone else.

I adopted a belief that I was alone in this business of paying for life's expenses. If I myself couldn't earn money, I knew I would end up on the streets, without food, and no protection. When money didn't come in like I expected (a late paycheck, a late client payment), I felt sick to my stomach even though there was always enough in my "envelopes."

Although I wrote and lived a different money story a long time ago, for some reason, the City's "no" tapped into that old story and for a moment I was back at that kitchen table imagining the "envelope shuffle."

I like the new story I wrote a whole lot better. I'm going to choose to keeping re-telling my better-ending money story instead of the old one where there's never enough, to say nothing of having more than enough. I choose my new story, I definitely choose my new story.

## *When You Want to "Chuck it All"*

In the moment you commit to altering your life, you feel sort of "pumped" with the adrenaline of possibilities. But when you encounter that first uphill stretch, there's a huge temptation to find the nearest side road and hightail it back to the Path of Least Resistance and your old, comfortable life.

Come on—admit it, you've done it before. We all have.

- You knew the company was going through a merger and you began to draft a new resume. Now, you thought, you could finally get that dream job you've always wanted.

    **BUT** you never finished the resume. It felt too daunting to remember your previous job responsibilities, consolidate them into two pages, and write a cover letter guaranteed to get an interview. You decided it was just easier to wait and see what happens when the new company takes over.

- Your sixtieth birthday was approaching and you knew you should think about planning for retirement. You even created a retirement file folder, including the latest copy of your financial statement, a couple of articles about enticing travel opportunities, and a bucket list of things you want to do when you have all that free time.

    **BUT** then you shared your thoughts with your spouse and were surprised to find that you had conflicting ideas about how you each wanted to live after retirement. You hate conflict so you dropped the subject and told yourself you'd get back to it in a year or two, or when she changes her mind.

- Your daughter was getting married in September and you knew what you had to do to lose the twenty pounds that would make you feel good about yourself as you walked her down the aisle. You went on a low-carb diet—that always worked for you before—and, for two weeks, you went to the gym every day.

    **BUT** then you had a piece of cake at your friend's fortieth birthday party. You went into that old mental tailspin, "Oh my god, I'm such a loser. I never follow through on anything; I guess I'm never supposed to be lovely or proud. Losing weight just isn't going to happen." So instead of getting right back on your weight-loss plan, the next day you buy a larger dress in a drab color that won't draw attention to your size.

You knew, and yet you didn't do. Or more likely, you did do, but only for a short time or until you hit the first bump in the road. Then you stopped, veered off course, and took a side road back to that familiar, but useless, Path of Least Resistance. You never, ever went all the way to the end. Why? Why do you keep doing that? What's missing?

In the past your M.O. has been to make a list and prioritize your goals, dreams, and projects. Putting them on paper served a comforting purpose; just looking at that organized list made you feel as if you were on your way to accomplishing everything. But

I'll bet that very little actually happened. More than likely, months later you found that list under a pile of papers, shook your head, and threw it out.

You're not alone in the habit of making lists and promises to yourself and never accomplishing what you set out to do. The corporate world is resolute about creating mission statements, company policy manuals, department goals and objectives, and five-year growth plans. Yet, I've coached many executives and company employees who can't repeat their company mission statement and have no idea what their department objectives are. Once the words were put to paper they were all but forgotten.

Listen, wishful thinking and dreaming is not now, and never has been, enough to keep you on course. At best it keeps you looking at, talking about and imagining how nice it will be when you're finally living your idyllic destiny. But the reality is that you're still "in neutral," doing the same things, being the same person, and dreaming the same unfulfilled dream. Without a reinforcement strategy in place to sustain your motivation and action, you'll never get to the end.

## *Pedaling a One-Speed Bike on a Thousand-Mile Journey*

Most efforts to make a sustained and lasting change are analogous to pedaling a one-speed bike on a thousand-mile journey. The beginning of this marathon-like ride is exhilarating and exciting. You start pedaling—taking new actions—with unbounded vitality and it feels, for a while, like it's all downhill. But the first time you

## Write an Empowering Story

hit a roadblock or the first time someone tells you that you're nuts, you'll, yet again, stop pedaling and abort the trip.

There's no way you'll ever complete a journey to enhance the quality of your life with just a self-pedaling, one-speed vehicle and an obscure inkling of where you're heading. Two crucial missing elements in this journey analogy are a personalized GPS-like **guide** for your self-directed walk toward your Ideal Destiny and high-octane, super-charged **fuel**—a mixture of passion, spirit, and motivation—needed for sustainability and uphill climbs.

Simply put, to complete any transformational journey, it's essential that you have:

Crystal Clear Destiny + Personal GPS + Super-Charged Fuel

or

Facts + Actions + Passion

or

Mind + Body + Heart

*"There is no right or wrong way to tell your improved story.... Just remember that the story you tell is the basis of your life. So tell it the way you want it to be."*

—*Abraham Hicks*

### *Write a New, Uplifting Life Story*

You can pump up your passion and create a personal GPS-like guide in one fell swoop by writing a better-feeling, engaging life story or, if you're the visual type, designing an inspiring vision board. I can't emphasize this enough: writing and telling a "wiser" story about your life is the single most powerful thing you can do to take this journey to its end where it finally all comes together.

"Come on Jo Anne, do I really have to write an actual story? I just want to get on with my journey and my life."

It's your choice, all your choice. Either you'll stride forward to living an enjoyable, satisfying, fulfilling life or you'll revert to living out an unfulfilling story from your past.

New and improved vs. old and unsatisfactory?
Your Choice!

COACHING NOTE:

Don't **think**, "I can't do this."

Don't **say**, "This is crazy."

Don't **put** this down and abort your desires yet again.

Lobotomize or banish or boot out any belief you have that writing a story is difficult or that you've never been a good writer. It doesn't have to be a perfectly designed composition and no one is going to correct it or critique it. You can compose it using any format that's easy for you. Type it in your computer or handwrite it in a journal, tell it to a trusted friend or coach who can write down the highlights for you to fill in later, or verbally record it on your computer or smartphone. There's no time limit. But, the sooner it's written, the sooner it can be used as one of your most vital tools for staying on course.

## Guide for Writing Your Uplifting Story

Since you always have a choice about your thoughts and feelings, decide up front to make the process of writing your better-feeling story a pleasurable experience. Have fun with this story writing exercise by including everything and anyone you want and excluding anything and anyone you don't want. Do you enjoy how you're valued in your morning coffee group? Include more of those types of experiences. If the guy next to you at work is a pain in the butt because of the stupid things he says, don't include him or anyone like him in your story. Do you absolutely love alone time? Make sure it's included. Do you feel invigorated by athletic activities? Make them a part of your story. Do you like to sleep late or get up early? Decide the exact time you want to open your eyes. Amplify and embellish all the details of every person, experience, feeling, adventure, or environment in your narrative until you have a story that calls to you and is inviting in every way.

> *Life-Design Journal page 230: If you've worked along with the chapters in this book, writing this uplifting story is almost complete. Use the play components from Chapter 2 as your outline. As the creator of your idealized story, you'll have total artistic license as set designer, casting agent, costumer, playwright, producer and director. To help fill in the broad categories of your story, refer to the components of your "Ideal Destiny" from pages 218 to 228 for your setting, ancillary characters, and ending. From pages 202 and 203, use the thoughts, words, and actions to create your dialogue and direction.*

## *Real-life Illustration:*
**Richard's Old Story:**

When I first met Richard, his days were filled with ongoing dissatisfaction and unhappiness with his business. He blamed the company's lack of growth *(the trigger)* on his unmotivated employees *(his belief)*. The result of repeating his they-are-to-blame story eventually seeped into his home life, his relationships with his family, his sense of self, and his health. I asked him what he really wanted, and he said he wanted his "ungrateful employees to realize they were lucky to have a job and to quit complaining when he asked them to work late." "After all," he said, "I'm paying them a lot of money and I seem to be the only one who works 24/7 around here *(thoughts and words)*."

After working together for a while, Richard came to realize that the running thread in his current story was the blame he placed on his employees. He saw that he never took any responsibility for his role in "this mess." I asked Richard to write a better-feeling story that didn't have as its central theme the placing of blame on anyone. He was asked to write a story that included his vision of an ideal business as well as his ideal life outside of that business.

## Write an Empowering Story

**Richard's Written Better-Feeling Business and Life Story**

"I own a manufacturing firm that was handed down to me from my grandfather. I have one hundred twenty employees and worldwide contracts. My company is profitable and my employees are happy to work here. Everyone is willing to take on new challenges and often make outstanding suggestions. I feel comfortable delegating projects. I now have more time to focus on other ideas for business growth. What I most like is that I have more time for my family and myself.

"My wife, Carrie, and I have been married for twenty-six years. We have a son named Tim and a daughter named Sue. My parents live in Arizona and I see them a couple of times a year. I'm not a deeply religious man, but I'm a good man. I believe in and live the Golden Rule. My friends say I'm deliberate and think things through before I answer; that's why they like to come to me for advice.

"I went to school to study architecture but I gave it up to join the family business. Lately I find that I feel the draw to use my design skills. One of my favorite pastimes is to stroll around new cities staring at the architectural nuances of the buildings and imagining how I would have sketched them if I'd been given the chance.

"I like to read, hike, scuba dive, and eat out in ethnic restaurants. Currently I'm designing a family getaway cabin that will have a gazebo over the stream. I enjoy my business and life a whole lot more, and am committed to continuing the journey."

**Richard's New Script Derived from His Story:**
"Hi Helen, how was your weekend?"

"Jim, can you come into my office. I liked that suggestion you made last week and want to know more about it. I think we can make that work."

"No I won't be in on Monday, we're going up north to our cabin."

"Did you hear about Sue's three goals in her last game? My daughter is a rock star."

"Yeah, I'm cutting back to working thirty hours a week. Frank's a good foreman and Miriam runs the office efficiently. I have nothing to worry about when I am not there. So why not?"

"Our trip to the Cayman Islands was great. Now that the whole family scubas, we are looking forward to our next adventure. I sure had a great time with the kids."

**Richard's Current Destiny:**
At this time, Richard is now living about 80% of that better-feeling story. These are the actual results of the changes that Richard has made:

His company is a short twenty-minute drive from his home. He has a bright office space that looks out on a stand of fir trees and a small lagoon. He recently changed the configuration in his office so he could see and be seen. His desk is a bit cluttered but that is how he works the best. All the employees have comfortable and clean work areas. This has become a priority of Richard and his managers. They noticed how much the chaos in the plant changed once the work areas were organized and personalized.

The changes he made in the company last year resulted in a 20% net increase while allowing him to spend 25% fewer hours at the office. He has de-hired employees that were in the wrong job for their skills, replacing them with competent, well-suited employees. The most noticeable leadership change has been Richard's willingness to delegate and listen. Since he has trained his managers well and is confident that they can make decisions that he will support, Richard doesn't have to be in the office every minute. With the release of worrying and obsessiveness, he now has time to spend with his family and to enjoy diving and hiking again.

When he gets to work, Richard makes it a point to greet each person he sees. He realized that acknowledging their presence was a big deal to them when he reviewed the results of his yearly "How can we be better for our customers and ourselves" survey. Once a year he takes each employee to lunch to get to know him or her better. He learned that one employee wanted to go back to school to be an architect. Imagine that? One wanted to take his wife to Great Britain to see the English gardens. One woman dreamed about putting an addition on her house to hold tutoring classes for neighborhood children at night.

After hearing their personal stories and dreams, he viewed each employee differently. Now when he greets them, he asks about their trip to England, or the addition to the house or the evening architecture classes. Suddenly—what a surprise!—his employees show up differently. The internal chaos is waning and profits are going up. He really likes his business environment.

Using the same formula, he then turned his focus to his customers. He got to know them, found out what made them get up each day, and asked about their families. Customer service became a pleasurable experience and, again, profits increased. Richard's employees and customers stay loyal to him and the company because he truly cares about their well-being.

Richard also spends more time with his children. He listens more than he speaks. And lately the kids share things that, in the past, he would have heard about only months after they happened. He goes to his daughter's soccer game every week and has started to take scuba lessons with his son. The family is planning a two-week scuba trip to the Cayman Islands in summer. His wife Carrie says that she is glad to have her husband back. Last weekend Richard and Carrie went up north and stayed in that cabin that Richard built last year. Since both Carrie and Richard like to eat at ethnic restaurants they make it a point to check the restaurant reviews each Thursday to see if a new one has opened. They make a date to dine there the following week. Richard and Carrie have also started hiking again on Sunday mornings.

Richard's parents in Arizona are thrilled that he has more leisure time. Now, when he comes to visit he's not preoccupied thinking about work. And when he Skypes each month, they're delighted that he seems interested in their life and friends. Three days a week he meets Mike, his closest friend, at the gym for a game of racquetball. After five years the score is Richard 258 and Mike 345. Richard is determined to even the score before the end of the year.

## *Giving Life to Your Life Story*

It's not enough to write a new story and lay it on top of your to-get-back-to pile of papers. That's akin to buying a seed packet and laying the unopened packet on top of the soil. Nothing will happen. Nothing will change. Nothing will grow. To pump energy and life into your script, it has to be "acted out." As you know, the path to a new destiny requires not only a change in thoughts and words, but also deliberate movement out of your comfort zone as you engage in new actions and behaviors.

And the first action I suggest is to devote ten minutes a day, for three months, to re-read your story or, if you created a vision board, to contemplate the pictures on your board. Thinking back to the life-as-a-play analogy, when actors are cast in a new play, they have to read the script over and over until they feel its intention and are able to grasp its life energy. Then, once they're connected to the intention and energy of the story, actors rehearse until they're comfortable with how their character moves about in the new scripted life.

Start rehearsing by making small behavior changes. Change a word, a thought, or an action. Wear a new "costume." Watch a different

TV show, go to a new restaurant, attend a lecture, meet someone new. You don't need to start by making big gestures or attempting major transformations. But, do something. Tell a portion of your new story to a casual acquaintance as if it has already happened. "Yes, I love to travel and will be going to Greece next year." "I'm so lucky to have young technology-savvy employees." "I'm working on the website for my new African import company." As you tell your story and act out your new behaviors, others will respond to their perception of you as that new character and will offer support to help you achieve your vision and dream. When before it seemed as if no one cared about your "someday" future, you'll now hear, "I have a friend who can help you, hire you, go with you, etc. Is there anything else I can do to help you?" If you're unsure what to rehearse, ask yourself, "In this new story what would my character think, say or do?" Then think, say, or do that one thing. Remember once your **Thoughts, Words,** and **Actions** are changed, new **Habits** will be formed. And, once that happens, your new **Character** will develop and the **Destiny**, which used to be just a wishful dream, will begin to materialize.

> *Life-Design Journal page 233: What days and times will you commit to reading, editing, and/or rehearsing your story for the next three months? Set your phone alarm with a special ringtone as a reminder. Develop a habit of reading your new story while you're on the treadmill, during your midmorning break, or last thing at night before you go to sleep.*

## Write an Empowering Story

You've ***explored*** your old stories and beliefs, ***liberated*** those you no longer wanted, and replaced them with others that were empowering. Then, you got clarity about what your idealized life looks like at this point in your life. Then to solidify the results of this work, you ***created*** a better-feeling life story. Does this mean you're now at the point of having a transformed life? Have you really found your true nature? Is this Utopia—the place where you can exhale and say, "Whew, I'm done; I've finally arrived?" Well not quite.

You see, you never permanently arrive and you're never done. If this journey has taught you anything, I hope it's taught you that life is one big luscious adventure. Your current Ideal Destiny is a jumping-off point for seeing the next horizon. You had to get here before you could see there. Whether on this journey, or on future journeys, when it's time to expand to your next horizon or alter your destiny, there will always be some devil on your shoulder tempting you to give up and stay right where you are; "Are you crazy? Your life is not that bad. Let well enough alone."

To deal with these nay-sayers in the last phase of this journey, Transformation, you'll design personal tools to keep you on course and steadily moving forward when people and/or events create seemingly insurmountably bumps in the road.

# TRANSFORMATION

# Chapter 12

## GETTING COMFORTABLE WITH BEING UNCOMFORTABLE

*From My Journal:*

    Today I'm facilitating a program for three hundred people and, for no apparent reason, I'm scared. What's this about? I really know what I'm talking about, have presented this topic many times before and will do well, as I always do.

    I'm remembering my first open-water dive trip in the Cayman Islands when I was nervous and scared—just like I am now. While our dive master, Danny, was giving the instructions for this dive, I was already in my mask, snorkel, and on the edge of the deck ready to jump in. I was too excited and scared to listen. I had a brilliant idea. I was going to swim right behind him once we got below the surface. He was the dive master; he knew what he was doing. So I couldn't go wrong by following him, could I?

    Off I went, over the side and down to the reefs. Half the group went to the left and I went to the right, three strokes behind Danny's butt. In no time we hit the reef and then I saw Danny dive downward. I followed right behind him. The next thing I knew, I was in a black hole and couldn't see one damn thing. Didn't know where to go, how to get out, and when I tried backing up, my tanks got caught on the top of the cave.

    My heart started pumping and I was rapidly using up oxygen. I was scared and didn't know what to do. But I did know. I told myself to calm down and breathe slowly and deeply. I knew that if Danny went in there, there must be a way out. I knew I could figure it out because I always somehow "figured it out."

    So I slowed my breath and then felt along the walls of the cave. I used the thing that was surrounding me as a guide to finding my way out. I stopped fighting it and started using it. I moved a bit to the right and I ran into wall, a bit to the left and ran into wall, a bit forward, and there was space. Bit by bit, I moved until it became apparent that there was eventually space to the left. In a few moments—seemed like hours—I saw a spot of light and kept moving toward it. Eventually I popped out of the black cave and there was Danny waiting for the other "expert divers" that he told to follow him down to the black hole. I sure got my butt chewed out when we got back aboard for not listening to his instructions that clearly indicated that this dive was only for experts.

But I learned a great lesson that day on what to do when I get scared and feel out of my depth. Breathe slowly, don't focus on what can go wrong, believe in my abilities to get myself out of the situation, remind myself of the lessons I learned, and instead of being encased by the problem, use its parameters as a guide to finding the way out.

> "It isn't the mountain ahead that wears you out—it's the grain of sand in your shoe."
>
> —Robert Service

### Here's That Mantra Again:

**"Nothing has meaning until I give it meaning."**

There is NOTHING that is inherently uncomfortable—or comfortable—for everyone. Your unique discomfort is "all in **your** head," the result of the hardwired, ongoing, repeated story of who you've been and how you've lived your life up until now.

Since you were a baby, you've had to learn new things and make changes thousands of times. Some you nailed right away. Others needed to be repeatedly practiced before you finally got it: tying your shoes, learning to type, putting on makeup, roller skating, driving a car. Some didn't work out at all: that dyed red hair, the claustrophobic factory job, living in the desert in summer. Simply put, that's just how you learned.

Each time you tried something new it was uncomfortable in the beginning, yet you kept going. So what is it about this particular "new journey" that has your undies in a bind and your "yeah-but" brain in full gear?

- I have no guarantee that I'm going to get there or will like it if I do.
- Why would I believe, that after so many previous attempts, I could do it now?
- What if I am chasing after rainbows? What if I'm making a fool of myself?

- What if I'm still not satisfied/happy/abundant/profitable/peaceful/calm/playful after I change?
- Will my family, friends, employees, and community still accept me?

Those fears come from that in-between place of, "I don't want to be the old habitual me but I only have a vague notion of who the new me is. And I don't know whether the work to get there is worth it or, honestly, if I have it in me to do it." You recognize that in order to have different, you have to **be** different. As I see it, the biggest obstacle to making a change is that before you do anything you want assurance that who you're going to become will be acceptable to everyone you know—including yourself. So, until you have that guarantee, you'll choose to keep both feet firmly glued in the past and just lean forward a little bit to see if you want to go further. Guess what: It just doesn't work that way.

## *Are You Ready to Be Different?*

"Yes I am, but, but... *There's a limit to what I can do and how I can change. I don't live in a vacuum. I have a family, co-workers, and a community to consider. And they're going to be very uncomfortable if I change. And besides,* **I** *just don't like feeling uncomfortable.*"

All those "buts" cement your feet in place because you choose to believe in their power. In essence you're giving "but" the meaning that: **Other's discomfort and/or my discomfort means that I have no choice but to keep my feet stuck.**

### Unstick Your Feet
**Tip #1 for "I can't change because if I do, *they* will be uncomfortable."**

And you were taught that it isn't nice to make someone else uncomfortable, weren't you?

- You suggest an employee support program and you hear, "You can't be serious? The board will wonder about your commitment to the shareholders."
- "What do mean you're not coming to Thanksgiving dinner this year? Grandma counts on it. She'll be so disappointed."
- "You can't be a vegetarian; you know how Dad loves to grill on Sunday. If you don't eat his steak, he'll be so disappointed."

Let's be honest. Whose discomfort are you really worried about? Theirs? Or your discomfort imagining their discomfort? Who are "they" and why are you giving them the power to keep you stuck in what you imagine their story is of you?

- If you create a new company program that supports the employees and not just the bottom line, who **do you believe** will give you the most resistance?
- If you change your job title from CEO to beer brewer, who **do you believe** will stop socializing with you or will question your sanity?
- If you take up dancing, who **do you believe** will laugh, question, or ridicule you?

- If you decide to take a part-time job after you've already retired, who **do you believe** will say, "But I thought you said you never wanted to work again." Who will try to keep you in the box of, "Once you say it, you have to do it forever?"
- If you decide to pursue a career after your kids leave home, who **do you believe** will say, "But what about our committees; what if your children need you to babysit for their kids?"
- If you decide you don't want to be single any longer, who **do you believe** will say, "But you said you'd never get married again."

The fact is you're probably 80% more uncomfortable with their possible discomfort than with your own. That might have been your M.O. in the past, but it doesn't have to be now. In your new story you aren't held hostage by other people's discomfort or, for that matter, your own. And while we're looking at this, why are you assuming they won't embrace the new you? Do you think this is the first time they've handled change? Why are you keeping them stuck in your story of who they are and not allowing them to show up differently?

When you own the belief that you can't change if it makes others feel uncomfortable, what you're really saying is:

- "I believe I know exactly what others will think, what they'll say, and how they'll act if I change."
- "I believe 'their' comfort is more important than mine."
- "I believe 'they' will never change."

- "I believe it's selfish to think about myself before someone else."

Bottom line: To unstick your feet from "I can't change because they'll feel uncomfortable," you need to acknowledge that "their stuff" is really all your own stuff.

> Life-Design Journal page 234: Whose discomfort are you most concerned about? What beliefs do you have about causing anyone to feel uncomfortable?

**Tip #2 for "I don't like feeling uncomfortable."**

Okay, that's easy to fix; **learn** to feel comfortable with being uncomfortable.

"*Oh my god, Jo Anne, I don't even want to think about living that way!*"

"*Okay, don't. Now, how do you feel?*"

"*Comfortable!*"

"*Sure you do. But how long is that going to last?*"

I'd be willing to bet that you learned to "avoid discomfort at all costs." The prudent people in your life told you: "Don't climb that tree, you'll get hurt." "Don't dream of living in a house like that, you'll only be disappointed." "Don't go to art school, you'll never make any money." "You want to quit your job? Are you nuts? You have a steady income so suck it up. In twenty-five years you'll have a pension."

Ergo, you did any and everything to avoid feeling uncomfortable. You've kidded yourself, promised yourself, blamed circumstances, the

## Getting Comfortable with Being Uncomfortable

economy, others, society, your neighbors, kids, spouses, co-workers, everyone and everything. You "chickened out" or "rationalized it" in the past. Has anything changed? Do you feel any better about your life, your business, your relationship, your career, your self-esteem, your age, or your dreams? No, you just felt comfortable in a cocooned speck of a moment. You crawled back in bed under a heavy comforter, again.

But now that you've done the work and have a picture of yourself living your Ideal-Someday-Life, and now that you've experienced excitement and passion about living in your new story, your comforter is never going to be heavy enough to silence that niggling, butt-kicking new voice of yours shouting, "Are you KIDDING me? You did all this work, finally figured out where you are going, got psyched about the reality that there is a path to achieving it, and you want to go take yet another trip back down that Path of Least Resistance? It never led us anywhere before. What **is** wrong with you?"

Answering in the background will be the muffled, fading voice from your old story, "Don't listen to her. You don't have to feel this way, you can't do it now, the boss is not in a good mood, you're moving and have no time, you have a headache, the dog is sick, it's tax time, the holidays are just around the corner.

Which voice are you going to listen to? Which voice are you going to give your energy to?

> *Life-Design Journal page 235: What does your play-it-safe voice say to you? What will your supportive voice need to say to prod you out from under the covers?*

## *Impulse Moments*

"Impulse Moment" is that brief iota of a moment when you experience the first hint of discomfort, when you hear an almost imperceptible "be-careful" warning or when you sense a subtle desire to regress to a comfortable-but-not-helpful behavior. It's in this exact moment that you have a choice to make. You can choose to give into the urge to crawl back under your comfort cover or you can decide to take a leap of faith. If you decide *not* to give in to your temptation, your focus will shift from instant gratification to long-lasting satisfaction. When you stop entertaining thoughts of your comfort zone and, instead, re-focus on your desired destiny, your discomfort immediately diminishes because you have ended the "in or out?" duel going on in your mind.

Remember Indiana Jones, the main character in the movie "Indiana Jones and the Last Crusade?" Jones was standing on the narrow edge of a deep chasm and knew that in order to save his dying friend, he had to get to the Holy Grail hidden in a cave on the other side. The riddle in the diary told him he must take a "leap of faith." So, with much trepidation, he stepped out into the void over the chasm. To his surprise his foot landed on a solid pathway leading to the other side. And, so will yours when you take a leap of faith on the first step on your Thoughtful Transformation Journey. Listen, this isn't the first time you've been faced with a situation where you didn't know beforehand what the exact outcome would be. Did you get through it? Sure you did. You're smart, have proven you're willing to do the work and have ventured down many new paths throughout your life. There's no reason you can't do it again.

*"A decision delayed until it is too late is not a decision; it's an evasion."*

—Anonymous

## Stay or Jump?

While you're contemplating your first step, consider that there are serious long-term effects to avoiding short-term discomfort:

- You'll have to take more and more "pain-killers" (i.e., your addictions) to avoid the discomfort.
- You'll stuff your desires so often that you'll convince yourself you never wanted them in the first place.
- You'll create illness and depression.
- You'll teach your children that it's not okay to look in another direction when the path they're on is not getting them where they want to go.
- You'll create rationalizing stories blaming others, society, timing, or any and everything for your inability to thoughtfully transform.
- You'll never enjoy the experiences on that list of incredible outcomes you associated with living your Ideal Destiny.

Remember Ellen's list of all she would give up if she stopped her journey? Re-read your own list on page 229. What happens if you, yet again, give into the discomfort, give up on your dreams, and return to the Path of Least Resistance? What price would you personally pay?

*"Okay, Jo Anne, I know the price I'll pay and that I need to value my comfort before others. It's not like I haven't tried this once or twice before. I get motivated, make lists and charts, and do really well for a day or two. Then the adrenaline subsides, I get really uncomfortable, go back to old behaviors and addictions, and it all falls apart. So how do I get beyond the discomfort?"*

Because you're traveling an unknown path with unknown hills to climb and unknown challenges to face, you'll be engaging unused muscles. Like any other unused physical muscles, your seldom-used mental, emotional, behavioral, and spiritual muscles may cramp or spasm until you stretch and strengthen them. Expect that there will be times when it doesn't feel natural and will therefore be uncomfortable. Don't run from the feeling. Eventually you'll become comfortable with being uncomfortable. After a while, you'll change change the *meaning* of discomfort from being a trigger to retreat to being a sign that you're moving in the right direction.

# Chapter 13

PREPLANNING SUPPORT
TO KEEP YOU ON COURSE

*From My Journal:*

One day when I was ten years old I came home for lunch shaking and crying.

During a catechism class when the priest asked if there were any questions, I raised my hand. "Who came first, Adam and Eve or the cavemen?" My question came from a purely observant fact that on my holy cards, Adam and Eve looked like they wore newer clothes than the hairy, gruff clothes that the cavemen wore in the pictures in my history book. I surmised that since the cavemen looked older, they must have come first.

What happened next was not fun. Literally, all hell broke loose.

The priest removed me from class and said he was shocked by my question. He told me I was a smart girl and should know better than to question the teachings of the church. He reminded me that excommunication could be the punishment for questioning those teachings. I knew what that meant. Sister had just told us that if anyone was excommunicated they were on a fast track to hell. The only way to repent was to go to Rome, walk on their knees across St. Peter's Square until they were bloody and then, after an appropriate amount of suffering and blood, beg to be personally forgiven by the Pope.

At lunch that day when Dad saw my tears, he assumed something horrendous must have happened to me. When I told him I needed money to go to Rome so I could appropriately bloody my knees and ask the Pope to forgive me, he started to laugh. To cover up, he said he was laughing because he was happy that this situation was something he could fix. I told him Sister told us only the Pope could fix the problem. What Sister didn't know, he told me, was that he "knew" the Pope.

Dad got up from the kitchen table and turned to the dial phone. After dialing a whole bunch of numbers he said, "Hello,

Pope. This is Frank Musolf." Then Dad told him my story. The next thing I heard was, "Thank you Pope. Yes, I'll tell Jo Anne that she doesn't have to worry but that she shouldn't tell Sister anything about our special arrangement because then Sister would have to let all the other Catholic kids in on the same deal."

When he got off the phone, Dad told me that the Pope said it was okay for me to ask questions and that I didn't need to come to Rome. The "pope" told Dad that he knew I was a smart girl and if I had any questions that I couldn't figure out I should have Dad call back anytime. I walked back to school after lunch with a smile on my face because my dad knew the pope, who was only a phone call away if I needed a reprieve.

After that initial "conversation" there were a few more pope-phone calls in the following years when I needed approval for thinking outside of the box or support for questioning the status quo. Now, when I'm unsure whether the path I'm heading down is going to bring me a whole lot of imagined backlash, I mentally pickup my cellphone and call the pope. He still says, "Go for it Jo Anne."

## *Don't Travel Alone*

Life isn't a do-it-yourself project; change isn't either. Staying on course will be easier if you set up support—people, places, activities, and objects—**in advance** for the times you sense that "Impulse Moment" when you want to chuck it all. Every person, every single person, who has made long-term successful changes pre-planned for "when I can't do it." Dieters keep fruit and nuts nearby, smokers have gum, TV addicts have books, workaholics "arrange" to have someone pick them up at work at a predetermined time, and couch potatoes get an exercise buddy.

**1. Support People**

Personal support can come from a coach, mentor, supervisor, friend, family member, or someone else on a similar journey. Maybe even from "the pope." However, it is imperative that whomever you enlist has no vested interest in where your journey leads you. Your support person's only goal should be your eventual happiness and contentment no matter where it takes you. Yes, it's important to get feedback and an occasional butt kick. But you don't want unsolicited opinions or advice from someone who doesn't want you to change because of how it will affect him/her.

Carefully select someone that appreciates how important this directional change is to you. Then call them—you can't just think about calling them—whenever you're feeling the tendency to give up or go off course. In the beginning set up a weekly appointment, coffee, workout, walk, or just a phone conversation to stay in touch and report on your Aha's and your Oh No's.

Years after clients have been well on their way to living their goals and dreams, many call every month or two for a thirty-minute reconfirming, reminding, or gentle butt kicking because I know the history of their journey, where they came from, where they want to go, and what obstacles seem to stop them in their tracks. The support people you choose need to be available for the long haul.

> *Life-Design Journal page 237: Who are your support people? Do they know where you want to go? What specific support will you need?*

### COACHING NOTE:

*Occasionally, clients balk at practicing the next section of their support plan by telling me they're too busy and can't possibly leave their desk or work space to get redirected. "Really," I respond. "If you had diabetes and needed an insulin shot, wouldn't you go to some other location to care for yourself? If you needed to make a very personal phone call, you'd remove yourself from your work area for privacy. Staying on this redirecting journey must be just as important to you as that life-supporting shot of medication or the much-anticipated response from that personal phone call." It's not crucial that all your pre-picked places are beautiful or exotic, but it is imperative that they be away from where you are in your moment of doubt or sabotage.*

## 2. Support Environment

A simple change of location or environment halts a run-amok mind and provides breathing space and re-focusing time. If you actually have the luxury of time at that moment, go to your pre-chosen spot for a "timeout." For some it may be a trip to a botanical garden, the gym, a café, the local coffee shop, a religious building, or a bookstore.

If your goal is to lose weight so you can enjoy physical activities, and you have a habit of repeatedly opening the refrigerator when you feel anxious, your alternative environment might be the front yard, where you'll weed the garden. Or you might take a stroll around the block or a trip to the garage where you'll sort your tools. If you're at work and can't get into a productive, peaceful rhythm because of negative conversation around you, leave your work space, go to the conference room, hallway, bathroom or to your car.

Once you're "there," wherever that may be, consciously breathe and become mindfully aware of your surroundings. Without judging, notice the trees, buildings or the feeling of the sun. Any act of conscious awareness pulls focus away from frustration and stops the downward spiral where, once again, you'll talk yourself into giving up or giving in.

> *Life-Design Journal page 237: Where are your "getaway" locations—at work and at home? What do you need to get away from when you are tempted to chuck it all?*

## 3. Support Activity

Any activity that's calming or elevates your spirits is a good choice for this solidifying phase of your change. Does it make you feel good to hit the trails for a run, putz in your garden, tinker with your car, attend a yoga class, go to a religious service, see a movie, try a new recipe, or explore a new neighborhood? Preplan this activity so you'll instinctively know what you're going to do when your old, out-of-date, mental messaging declares, "You can't do this, dummy."

If you're in a situation where you can't physically leave, click on your computer or smartphone and go to a website of a country you've always fancied visiting, repeat a mantra, sing an uplifting song in your head, or simply put in ear buds and listen to a piece of energizing or tranquil music.

> *Life-Design Journal page 238: What activities, both physical and mental, do you have at the ready to keep you calm, focused, and off the edge?*

## 4. Support Objects

Hang, tape, or carry a picture as a visual reminder of your life to come. Some clients create full vision boards using magazine clippings to represent visuals of their exciting ideal life. Some design a screensaver with a motivational saying or a photo of why they're doing this work. Carry motivational books in your car, in a travel bag, or download them to your e-reader. As you eat lunch, have afternoon coffee, take a work break, or drive home from work, use these books and tapes to keep yourself "juiced." Every week put fresh flowers on your desk or in your house as a reminder that your life is in bloom. Read your "What I'll Miss Out On If I Don't Go the Distance" list and incorporate one new experience into your life each week.

> *Life-Design Journal page 238: What visual reminders or objects will you use to support you on this journey? What reminders, pictures, or objects will you remove that keep you stuck in the past?*

### 5. Create a Destiny Mini-Reminder

On one side of a note card, or on your smartphone or tablet list the three or four most meaningful and captivating aspects of your newly designed destiny. Choose whichever dreamed-about outcomes garner the biggest smile. On the other side, note the three or four things you'll regret not doing or experiencing if you give into your discomfort or fear.

If your mini-reminder is a notecard, make duplicate copies to put one in your wallet or purse, put one near your computer, one on the console of your car, hang one on the mirror or refrigerator or place one anywhere else that'll catch your eye. Keeping features of your Ideal-Life vision and the experiences you'll forfeit for giving in to momentary doubt or discomfort in sight strengthens those comfortable-with-discomfort muscles that you'll need as you experience future changes in your life.

> *Life-Design Journal page 239: Create your Mini-Reminder. What's on the front of your card? What's on the back? Where will you place your cards?*

## 6. Jolt-Yourself-Awake Phrases

I've heard that when you have an emotionally charged thought, the energy from that thought takes six to twelve seconds to penetrate into the cells of your body. If it's a pleasing thought—that was fun, I really like my new job, this tastes awesome—positive energy flows. On the other hand, if it's an unpleasant thought—I feel like a loser, my boss just doesn't like me, I hate my thighs—negative energy invades your cells. Furthermore, whether the energy is positive or negative, it can stay in your body for up to ten hours and affect your experiences the rest of the day.

Therefore, preplan what technique or phrase you'll have in place to dissipate negative energy before it affects the quality of your experiences and the degree of "Okay-ness" you'll have in the following six to ten hours. The twelve seconds you have between thought and the flow of energy is more than enough time to pause, refocus, and get back on course.

The quickest way I know how to do this is to have a few phrases in my mental "Stop It" thesaurus that jolt me back to being the director of the quality of my life.

Some words and phrases I use are:

- Lobotomize it!
- That's not who I am!
- Cancel, cancel.
- Nope, not me!
- Are you kidding me?
- That's an old story.
- Shut up!
- It's just a thought; it's not true.
- Going backwards is NOT an option.
- This is just rehearsal, give me a break.

Mentally shout one of these phrases as soon as you're on the edge and know, that if you don't do something immediately, you're going to give in and go backwards:

- "I'm too old for this." **Lobotomize it!**
- "Nothing is ever going to change." **Cancel, Cancel!**
- "It's no use creating a new resume, they hire only young people." **That's not who I am!**
- "I tried to be different and I got a strange look." **This is just rehearsal, give me a break!**

An immediate, contrary, authoritative response to your defeating thought or words will stop the backward slide. Remind yourself that you're not that person anymore and that you're taking back control of your thoughts. Eventually, the power those self-defeating thoughts have over you will vanish, and the power you have over them will grow to the point that they will no longer be a part of your story.

*Life-Design Journal page 240:* What words or phrases will you use to stop a defeating thought, word, or action from taking hold and causing a backward slide?

*Life-Design Journal page 241: Specific Pre-Planning Needs:* Refer back to page 229 where you listed the benefits of living your ideal life and choose ten that you want to experience sooner than later. Next to each, indicate the kind of support you think you'll need and the person or organization you can call on for assistance.

# Chapter 14

## LIVING YOUR "SOMEDAY" NOW!

*From My Journal:*

Yesterday I got up from sleeping across the front seat of my van and drove to Acadia National Park to hike the kinks out of my body. While in the parking lot, I gazed at the top of Cadillac Mountain, which is supposed to be the first spot the sun hits the U.S. each morning. I thought, "Wouldn't it be fun to be the first person to see the sun someday?" But, viewed through my fear of heights, that mountain appeared pretty damn high.

While I was looking up, an elderly man (actually dressed in lederhosen) walked up to me and asked, "You've been staring at the top of the mountain for a while. What are you thinking, sweetheart?"

"Someday I'd like to be at the top to see the sun before anyone else."

"Then do it."

"Well, I'm not comfortable with heights. But when I am, I'll come back and do it."

"No you won't."

Then continuing he said, "I'd give anything for your youth and your health and all the times in my life I said 'someday.' You'll never be as young as you are and as healthy as you are right now."

Just then another man who was standing nearby said, "I overheard you talking. I'm a photographer and plan to hike to the top tomorrow morning to take pictures for my magazine. If you get here before the sun comes up, I'll take you to the top with me."

My wise, new friend then said, "Honey, looks like your 'Someday' is now!"

And so this morning, (after praying for rain all night long) I awoke to a clear, windless day and met that photographer to climb to the top. For so many reasons, today's sunrise was the most magnificent I've ever experienced.

"'Someday' is Now!" is going to be my nudging mantra from here on in.

*"The privilege of a lifetime is being who you are."*
—Joseph Campbell

## Your First Step

Although we're at the end of the book, you're at the starting point of your walk down the Path of Thoughtful Transformation, the path that will lead you toward the life, the career, the retirement, the relationship, the business, the health, or the peace of mind you've always said you wanted.

You explored the history and stories of who you've been and you've examined and released the useless "baggage" you've been carrying. You've learned how to question your conscious and unconscious beliefs, how to get clear about what you really want, how to write and rehearse living your Ideal-Life story, and how to equip yourself with support before you take the first step.

You also know that no matter how often you think you have the ultimate plan for living the rest of your life, in the not-too-far future you'll soon experience another trigger to make a life or business change. That's just the adventure of life. But this time when those triggers occur, you'll have done the work to use as a benchmark for making future decisions.

So, what are you waiting for? Just as my wise guru said to me that day at the base of the mountain, I say to you

**"Your 'Someday' is Now!"**

I sincerely thank you for reading this book and I applaud you for your courage to make transformative changes in your life. If anyone tells you you're crazy for trying to make your life better, don't listen to him or her. Lobotomize their negative energy. I personally support your every effort and look forward to hearing how your individual journey is progressing. You can email me at **joanne@joannemusolf.com** to share your efforts and results. If you include your email address (make sure it's correct and current) I will respond to everyone. Also, if you want information about my upcoming appearances or workshops and retreats I will be leading, check my website at **www.joannemusolf.com**. I look forward to meeting you some where and some how.

# _____'s Life-Design Journal

"*The biggest obstacle to any kind of transformation is the voice that tells you it's impossible.*"

—*Geneen Roth*

## EXPLORATION

The journey to making transformative changes begins by illuminating your legacy, stories and beliefs you're lugging around; identifying the event that triggered your desire to change; and determining your level of commitment to finish this journey to its end.

## *Chapter 1*

*"Restlessness and discontent are the first necessities of progress"*
—Thomas Edison

### WHAT'S YOUR TRIGGER FOR CHANGE?

**What would you like to change?** Review the charts on pages 9 and 10 and list each life and business category where you'd welcome an alteration or total change.

_____    _____
_____    _____
_____    _____
_____    _____
_____    _____
_____    _____
_____    _____

Return to page 7.

**Two or Three:** Which two or three of those that you just listed do you feel the strongest need or urge to change?

_____
_____
_____
_____
_____
_____

Return to page 7.

**What is your " The One" and why?** "The One" is the area you'll focus on at the beginning of your journey. The others you listed will be integrated in this transformational journey as you move closer to your goal.

**The One!** _____
_____
_____
_____
_____
_____
_____
_____
_____

Return to page 8.

**What is your Trigger:** Why now, at this particular time, do you feel compelled to make a change to your life or business? Describe your triggering experience. If you need more space continue on another sheet.

_____
_____
_____
_____
_____
_____
_____
_____
_____
_____
_____
_____
_____
_____
_____

Return to page 11.

**Pushed or Pulled:** Are you looking forward to this change, being forced to endure it, or feeling neutral about it? Write a few words about this feeling.

_____
_____
_____
_____
_____
_____

Return to page 12.

**Level of Urgency:** On scale of 1-10, with 10 being very motivated, what's your level of urgency? Write more about why you chose that number. Don't judge the number—it's only information.

**1-10** _____

_____
_____
_____
_____
_____
_____

Return to page 13.

**Level of Staying Power:** On a scale of 1-10, how likely are you to stay with this journey to the end? Why or why not? Again, don't judge the number you choose—it's just information.

**1-10** _____

_____
_____
_____
_____
_____
_____
_____
_____
_____
_____
_____
_____
_____
_____
_____

Return to page 13.

## Chapter 2

*"To reform a man you must begin with his grandmother."*
—*Victor Hugo*

### WHO'S REALLY TAKING YOUR JOURNEY?

**Your Life-Defining Play:** Using the prompted questions from the play categories in Chapter 2, fill in the specifics of your Life-Defining Play. As you continue your journey, you'll remember other events that defined your early life. Return to this journal section and add those new insights as they occur.

Living Your 'Someday' Now

## _____'S LIFE-DEFINING PLAY
*Insert Your Name*

**Lead Actor:** _____

**Setting and Context:** Use prompting questions from page 25.

_____

_____

_____

_____

_____

_____

_____

_____

_____

_____

_____

_____

_____

_____

_____

_____

_____

_____

_____

_____

**Supporting Cast of Actors:** Use prompting questions from page 25.

## Living Your 'Someday' Now

**Script:** Use prompting questions from page 26.

Life-Design Journal

**Director(s):** Use prompting questions from page 26.

**Character Development:** Use prompting questions from page 27.

# Life-Design Journal

**Costumes:** Use prompting questions from page 27.

_____
_____
_____
_____
_____
_____
_____

**Ending:** Use promtping questions from page 28.

_____
_____
_____
_____
_____
_____
_____
_____

Return to page 28.

## Chapter 3

*In regard to beliefs, Anthony Robbins, motivational speaker and coach, says: "More often than not, they can limit our vision of how we want to live, and unconsciously alter our level of achievement and happiness in life."*

**WHAT BELIEFS HAVE YOU BEEN LUGGING AROUND?**

**Your Beliefs:** Start a list of your beliefs—you'll add to it in future chapters. Include both the obvious and the obscure: *rules must always be obeyed, never jaywalk, a messy house is sign of a lazy person, older women shouldn't wear their hair long.* In the "Liberation" segment of your journey, you'll decide which life-defining beliefs you want to hold on to and which ones you want to boot out.

_____
_____
_____
_____
_____
_____
_____
_____
_____

# Life-Design Journal

Return to page 35.

**Programmed Beliefs:** What did the adults in your life teach you to believe? Pull ideas from the "Script" of your Life-Defining Play on page 190. If you still own those beliefs, add them to your belief list on page 195.

_____
_____
_____
_____
_____
_____
_____
_____
_____
_____
_____
_____
_____
_____
_____
_____
_____

Return to page 39.

**Exposure:** What beliefs or leanings did you adopt due to the era and/or environment you grew up in, i.e., during the Great Depression, the sixties, post 9-11? If you still own them, add them to your belief-list on page 194.

_____
_____
_____
_____
_____

Return to page 39.

**Experiences:** Which words, looks, comments, smells, titles, or numbers cause a spontaneous gut reaction? Can you extrapolate the belief behind that reaction? What impacting experiences affected your life? What beliefs resulted from those impacting experiences? Add these beliefs to your list on page 194.

_____
_____
_____
_____
_____

Return to page 41.

**Conscious Beliefs:** If asked, "Why can't you do what you say you want to do?" what would your immediate answers be? Add these beliefs to your list on page 194.

_____
_____
_____
_____
_____
_____
_____
_____
_____
_____
_____
_____
_____
_____
_____
_____
_____
_____
_____

Return to page 43.

**Unconscious Beliefs:** Do you have an instinctive reaction to a person, event, idea, smell, etc.? What is the reaction and where does it come from? What is the resulting belief you own?

_____
_____
_____
_____
_____
_____
_____
_____
_____
_____
_____
_____
_____
_____
_____
_____
_____
_____
_____
_____

Return to page 43.

**Truths:** What are your truths? What beliefs, philosophies, and tenets governs your life?

_____
_____
_____
_____
_____
_____
_____
_____
_____
_____
_____
_____
_____
_____
_____
_____
_____
_____
_____
_____

Return to page 45.

## Chapter 4:

"Freedom involves making decisions, and each decision is a destiny decision."

—Joseph Campbell

### WHY DO YOU KEEP ENDING UP AT THE SAME PLACE?

**A Road Map to a New Destiny**

Thoughts > Words > Actions > Habits > Character > Destiny

**Your Personal Road Map:** List a situation or experience you'd like to alter. Now, fit the specifics of your I-can't-do-it thinking into the T>W>A>H>C>D pattern. Use this Thought-to-Destiny pattern whenever you catch yourself thinking, saying, or doing anything non-supporting or not inline with the outcome you're pursuing.

**What situation would you like to alter?**

_____
_____
_____
_____
_____
_____
_____

**Thoughts:** What "thought(s)" do you repeatedly have regarding this situation?

_____
_____
_____
_____
_____
_____
_____
_____

**Words:** What "words" do you repeatedly use when talking about this situation?

_____
_____
_____
_____
_____
_____
_____
_____.

**Actions:** What "actions" do you take or not take based on those thoughts and words?

_____
_____
_____
_____
_____
_____
_____
_____

**Habits:** List your conscious habits surrounding this situation.

_____
_____
_____
_____
_____
_____
_____
_____
_____
_____

**Character:** How do you characterize yourself? How do you think others characterize you in regards to this situation?

_____
_____
_____
_____
_____
_____
_____
_____

**Destiny:** Looking at your answers to the above five questions, in one sentence describe your current life destiny.

_____
_____
_____
_____
_____
_____
_____
_____

Return to page 60.

## Chapter 5

*"I'm a slow walker, but I never walk back."*

—*Abraham Lincoln*

### WHICH PATH WILL YOU CHOOSE?

**Path of Least Resistance:** What pain-avoiding, anesthetizing, or repeating behavior do you use? What's your first action, your first thought, or the first words out of your mouth when you're feeling uncomfortable? What's the first thing you're inclined to do?

_____
_____
_____
_____
_____
_____
_____
_____
_____
_____
_____
_____
_____
_____

## Living Your 'Someday' Now

_____

_____

_____

_____

_____

_____

_____

Return to page 68.

**Path of Thoughtful Transformation:** Reflecting on your level of urgency from page 185, record any thoughts you have about this path taking longer to travel or being a bit weird. Also, include any gut reactions to not having your pain-avoiding, anesthetizing, or repeating behaviors to use when you feel uncomfortable.

_____

_____

_____

_____

_____

_____

_____

Return to page 72.

## LIBERATION

*Chapter 6*

*When you don't know what to do next, dance!*

*—Jo Anne Musolf*

### *STOP!* DON'T DO ANYTHING

The first step on the transformation journey is actually a non-step. Just stop for a moment to let the work you've done so far settle in. I suggest that today, instead of writing in this journal, call a friend to engage in a feeling-good activity. Take a few hours to experience some of the benefits of living a thoughtful, transformed life.

**What did you do?**

_____
_____
_____
_____
_____
_____
_____
_____

Return to page 78.

## Chapter 7

*"In the long run men only hit what they aim at."*
—Henry David Thoreau

### WHAT DO YOU REALLY WANT?

What are your **Aha's?** To get to the truth of what your heart, mind, and soul *really want* and to liberate your "Aha's," answer the four Destiny-Clarifying questions.

**What don't you want?**

_____
_____
_____
_____
_____
_____
_____
_____
_____
_____
_____
_____

**Based on those answers, what do you *allegedly* want?**

_____
_____
_____
_____
_____
_____
_____
_____

**Why do you want what you want?**

_____
_____
_____
_____
_____
_____
_____
_____
_____

**And why do you want those things?**

_____
_____
_____
_____
_____
_____
_____
_____

**And why those things?**

_____
_____
_____
_____
_____
_____
_____
_____
_____

Life-Design Journal

**Now, what do you really want?**

Return to page 90.

## Chapter 8

*"Thinking about the right thing to do often gets in the way of doing it right."*

—Sue Bender

### WHY DON'T YOU ALREADY HAVE WHAT YOU WANT?

**Why Don't You Have It?** For each of your answers to "What do you really want?" on page 211, extrapolate the limiting belief that's keeping you stuck.

*I really want:* _____
*But:* _____
*But:* _____

*I really want:* _____
*But:* _____
*But:* _____

*I really want:* _____
*But:* _____
*But:* _____

*I really want:* _____
*But:* _____
*But:* _____

Return to page 98.

## Chapter 9

### METAPHORICALLY *"LOBOTOMIZE"* LIMITING BELIEFS

**Destiny-Diverting Belief #1:** What do you believe is unchangeable or insurmountable in your life, with another person, or concerning a specific situation?

_____
_____
_____
_____
_____
_____
_____
_____
_____
_____
_____
_____
_____
_____

Return to page 106.

**Destiny-Diverting Belief #2:** List at least five times you've made changes or learned new skills that were enjoyable experiences. When you're tempted to go down the "I hate changing and I'm going to stop now" spiral, you can refer to these experiences to break that useless thought pattern.

**Enjoyable learning and changing experiences:**

_____
_____
_____
_____
_____

Return to page 107.

**Destiny-Diverting Belief #3:** Write about a time when you downplayed feeling joyful or when you minimized a successful business outcome because you thought if you made yourself seem "less than" or "not okay" it would make someone else feel better.

_____
_____
_____
_____
_____

Return to page 108.

**Uncover, Lobotomize, and Update Your Beliefs:** Practice this exercise by stating one thing you've always wanted or one thing you'll regret not experiencing. Take time as you go through each step. Pay close attention to the **words, thoughts,** and **actions** you're using to rationalize why you don't already have what you want. Then, be equally thoughtful about replacing them with alternatives that are empowering and supportive.

**I want:** _____
_____

1. **State why you don't already have what you want.**

_____
_____
_____
_____
_____

2. **List your beliefs based on the statements you just made.**

_____
_____
_____
_____
_____

3. Declare those beliefs "lobotomized" and replace them with new empowering beliefs.

_____
_____
_____
_____
_____
_____
_____
_____
_____
_____

4. If you "owned" those new empowering beliefs, what would you think, say, and do (T>W>A) differently?

_____
_____
_____
_____
_____

5. If you're resistant to taking any of those actions or adopting the replaced empowering beliefs, start over with #1.

Return to page 114.

# CREATION

## *Chapter 10*

### WHAT ELSE IS ON YOUR BUCKET LIST?

**Your Bucket List:** Use the questions posed in Chapter 10 as a guide to create a draft of what your "Ideal Destiny" might look like if you had it all. Sit with your idealized destiny for a few days. Then return to these pages and re-examine your answers. Add to, delete, or edit as you gain new insight.

1. **Leisure: (page 125)**

_____

_____

_____

_____

_____

_____

_____

_____

_____

_____

_____

_____

2. **Education/Learning: (page 126)**

## Life Style: (page 126)

# Life-Design Journal

3. **Geography/Environment: (page 126)**

**4. Civic Engagement/Volunteer: (page 126)**

Life-Design Journal

5. **Career: (page 127)**

6. Health/Wellness: (page 127)

Life-Design Journal

7. **Identity: (page 127)**

8. **Life purpose: (page 128)**

Life-Design Journal

## 9. Relationships: (page 128)

**10. Money/Abundance: (page 128)**

Return to page 129.

**Benefits of Living Your Ideal Destiny:** Extrapolate the benefits of living your Ideal Destiny by finishing this sentence: "If I give up the me I know I want to be and the life I want to live, I give up the following…" You'll refer back to this list later when you create a plan for the support you'll need as you continue on your journey.

## Chapter 11

"Regardless of circumstance, each man lives in a world of his own making."

—Josepha Murray Emms

### WRITE AN EMPOWERING STORY

#### COACHING NOTE:

*I recommend handwriting your story on a separate sheet of paper. The process of putting pen to paper engages a rhythm and energy where the story sort of begins to write itself. If you absolutely hate the idea of handwriting, type it into your computer.*

**Your Better-Feeling Story:** If you've worked along with the chapters in this book, writing this uplifting story is almost complete. Use the play components from Chapter 2 as your outline. As the author of your idealized story, you'll have total artistic license as set designer, casting agent, costumer, playwright, producer and director. To help fill in the broad categories of your story, refer to the components of "Ideal Destiny" from pages 218 to 228 for your setting, ancillary characters, and ending. From pages 202 and 203 use the thoughts, words, and actions to create your dialogue and direction.

Life-Design Journal

∽ ∽ ∽

I have included another client example to assist you in writing your story. Brian found it easier to write his Ideal Life story in the third person. Here is his self-authored better-feeling story:

### The Story of Brian the Artist

Don't say it's too late for anything. Brian Smith is an artist who has changed his life and career many times.

He and Adrienne moved to Europe to be near the water, the culture, and the people. Brian has built quite a unique living space for them. Their "home" is right on the water. There is a stand of trees/bushes on the front of the property along the beach. They have a walkway from the property to the beach that they travel each day to watch sunrises/sunsets and take walks.

Brian and Adrienne live in two separate structures on either side of a common courtyard with a fireplace, flowers, and comfortable chairs and tables for conversations and reading. Brian's house/studio is two stories. He sometimes lives in the upper half with a bedroom, office, bath and kitchen/living area. There is a large window where he can see the ocean and a balcony off the living space. Downstairs is his art studio that has a large glass sliding door leading to his private personal patio, where he can store stuff or do whatever the hell else he wants with it. In the back of his "piece of paradise" he has a workshop for woodworking, etc. He foresees a time in the near future where he has 2-3 on-call employees who do the basic woodworking, run into town for supplies etc.

Brian loves the fact that with a living/working area separate from Adrienne's he can make as much of a mess as he wants and he won't interfere with her organized, clean living area. Brian sees Adrienne's house as big enough to have all the room she wants, including a guest room and a large garden in both the front and back yards. They both work in the garden at times.

When he gets up in the morning, Brian puts on his work jeans, grabs a cup of coffee and walks to the ocean to smell the air, hear the birds and begin his day. What he likes most about his lifestyle here is that he has no restrictions on his time unless they are self-imposed. He gets up when he wants, take naps when he wants, and doesn't have to answer to anyone unless he wants. If he is working on an art piece or another project, he may "hibernate" for days at a time and work as long into the night as he wants.

It takes Brian about 15 minutes to drive his truck into town, which has supplies, stores, movies, culture, cafes, art shows, museums, festivals, swap meets, and a farmer's market.

With the airport and train station less than an hour away he takes trips (sometimes alone) to other European towns and villages to explore and experience the area's attractions

# Life-Design Journal

and people. He's been to Africa and all over Europe. He particularly loves the street vendors, local markets, cobblestone street, shops, cathedrals, museums, and street cafes.

Although Brian spends some time on his artwork, with his doctorate in physics (theoretical and experimental), he consults on selected projects. As a matter of fact, he is working on a project now that, because of his thesis, may earn him a nomination for a Nobel Prize. As part of an Art Association, his work is marketed and sold across Europe.

Tom, Brian's brother, recently moved to the area and lives not far from their house. Sometimes Brian and Tom go backpacking and explore the local trails. Once a year Brian goes back to the United States to visit his family and friends.

**Your Commitment:** What days and times do you commit to reading, editing, and/or rehearsing your story for the next three months? Set your phone alarm with a special ringtone as a reminder. Create a habit of reading your new story while you're on the treadmill, during your mid-morning break, or last thing at night before you go to sleep.

_____

_____

_____

_____

Return to page 148.

# TRANSFORMATION

## Chapter 12

*"The diamond cannot be polished without friction, nor the man perfected without trials."*

—Chinese proverb

**GETTING COMFORTABLE WITH BEING UNCOMFORTABLE**

**How to Unstick Your Feet:**
**Tip #1:**
Whose discomfort are you most concerned about?

_____
_____
_____
_____
_____
_____
_____
_____
_____
_____
_____
_____

What beliefs and stories do you have about causing someone's discomfort?

_____
_____
_____
_____
_____
_____
_____
_____

Return to page 160.

**Tip #2**

What does your play-it-safe voice say to you?

_____
_____
_____
_____
_____
_____
_____
_____

What will your supportive voice need to say to prod you out from under the covers?

_____
_____
_____
_____
_____
_____
_____
_____

Return to page 162.

## Chapter 13

*"Instead of crying over spilled milk, go milk another cow."*

—Erna Asp

### PREPLANNING SUPPORT TO KEEP YOU ON COURSE

**Support People:** Who are your support people? Do they know where you're going? What specific support will you need?

_____
_____
_____
_____

Return to page 169.

**Support Environment:** Where are your "getaway locations—at work and at home? What do you need to get away from when you are tempted to chuck it all?

_____
_____
_____
_____

Return to page 170.

**Support Activity:** What activities, both physical and mental, do you have at the ready to keep you calm, focused, and off the edge?

_____
_____
_____
_____
_____
_____
_____

Return to page 171.

**Support Objects:** What visual reminders or objects will you use to support you on this journey? What reminders, pictures, or objects will you remove that keep you stuck in the past?

_____
_____
_____
_____
_____
_____
_____

Return to page 172.

**Create a Destiny Mini-Reminder:** Create your Mini-Reminder. What's on the front of your card? What's on the back? Where will you place your cards?

_____
_____
_____
_____
_____
_____
_____
_____
_____
_____
_____
_____
_____
_____
_____
_____
_____
_____

Return to page 173.

Living Your 'Someday' Now

**Jolt-Yourself-Awake Phrases:** What words or phrases will you use to stop a defeating thought, word, or action from taking hold and causing a backward slide?

_____
_____
_____
_____
_____
_____
_____
_____
_____
_____
_____
_____
_____
_____
_____
_____
_____
_____

Return to page 175.

Life-Design Journal

**Specific Pre-Planning Needs:** Refer back to page 229 where you listed the benefits of living your ideal life and choose ten that you want to experience sooner than later. Next to each, indicate the kind of support you think you'll need and the person or organization you can call on for assistance.

1. _____   _____
2. _____   _____
3. _____   _____
4. _____   _____
5. _____   _____
6. _____   _____
7. _____   _____
8. _____   _____
9. _____   _____
10. _____   _____
11. _____   _____
12. _____   _____
13. _____   _____
14. _____   _____
15. _____   _____
16. _____   _____
17. _____   _____
18. _____   _____
19. _____   _____
20. _____   _____

## Chapter 14

*"One of these days" is none of these days.*

—Anonymous

### LIVING YOUR "SOMEDAY" NOW!

I sincerely thank you for reading this book and I applaud you for your courage to make transformative changes in your life. If anyone tells you you're crazy for trying to make your life better, don't listen to him or her. I personally support you're every effort and look forward to hearing how your individual journey is progressing. You can email me at **joanne@joannemusolf.com**. If you include your email address—make sure its correct and current—I will respond to everyone. Also, if you want information about up-coming appearances I will be making or workshops and retreats I will be leading, check my website at **www.joannemusolf.com**.

# ABOUT THE AUTHOR

Twenty years ago after many years as a business executive, a company CEO, a Vice President of National Sales and an International Sales Manager, Jo Anne Musolf, took a look at her life and said, "Wait a minute, why am I doing all this? When am I going to start living the life I have been working so damn hard to have?"

Her answer was, "NOW"

Jo Anne's desire to assist and support individuals aspiring to make both personal and professional changes in their life led her to become a international coach, consultant, and, as her friends say, "meddler" specializing in changes and transitions.

In addition to her consulting and coaching, Jo Anne has authored numerous articles, been a frequent guest on radio and TV shows, and delivered seminars and keynote speeches around the world.

If you ask JoAnne what she needs that she doesn't have, she'll look at you with a quizzical smile. Then she'll respond, "Well, at this moment I can't think of anything. I love my life and my business. I'm content. But I expect that at any given moment either my life or business circumstances will change. When they do, I know that I'll always find my way to the next destination."

JoAnne is a product of her own process.

Her "Someday..." is always today

www.ingramcontent.com/pod-product-compliance
Lightning Source LLC
Chambersburg PA
CBHW070558300426
44113CB00010B/1309